KEYS TO SUCCESSFUL
PIANO LESSONS

D1202611

KEYS TO SUCCESSFUL PIANO LESSONS

by
Mary Teel Johnson

The Performing Arts Lodge
110 The Esplanade
Toronto, Ontario *Withdrawn*
Lpt 2023

Somma
Seaside, California

© Copyright 1987 by Mary Teel Johnson
All rights reserved.

First Printing January 1987
Second Printing June 1987
Third Printing January 1990

Library of Congress Cataloging in Publication Data

Johnson, Mary Teel
    Keys to Successful Piano Lessons

Library of Congress Catalog Card No. 87-158781
ISBN #0-943021-01-4

Published by Somma Distributing, Seaside, CA 93955
Printed in the United States of America

Dedicated to my husband, who always understood, and encouraged my love affair with the piano.

ACKNOWLEDGEMENTS

My thanks and acknowledgements to Steinway & Sons who permitted the use of Steinway photographs to illustrate the various size pianos; to Sidney Harris who permitted me to quote his article on "What Is Great Music;" and to my editor, Elaine Funchess-Jones of Carmel, California, for her excellent editing and encouragement for this book.

TABLE OF CONTENTS

PREFACE

PART I: THE STUDENT

PART II: THE TEACHER

PART III: THE INSTRUMENT

PART IV: THE LESSONS

CONTENTS

PART V: BEYOND THE BASICS

PREFACE

You are reading this book for one of two reasons: you want to start your child on piano lessons, or you wish him to continue taking lessons. You want to examine your reasons, find out what to expect from a course of instruction, what is required of you, the parent, as well as your child, the student.

The observations and opinions in this book are based on 45 years of teaching piano to students of all ages. Conversations with parents during these years indicated a need for such a guide. This book addresses the many questions that make the role of parent more informed, thus easier.

The initial decision to expose a child to piano lessons is made for a wide variety of reasons. Here are some of the least effective reasons parents have for wanting lessons for a child:

—"I always wanted to take piano lessons, so I want to make sure my child gets to."

—"A friend is storing his piano with us, and it seems a shame not to use it."

There are better reasons: ideally, the child has expressed a wish to play a musical instrument, particularly the piano. Perhaps he has demonstrated a fascination with sounds, or has picked out little tunes on a piano in your home. Often a child has heard a friend play and wants to try it too. This desire to learn, either natural to the child or engendered by his parents, is necessary for success.

In the case of the older student, one who is beyond the basics, the decision to continue lessons poses different questions. Usually young adults are self-motivated. If they no longer want to take lessons, forcing them to continue may be an exhausting battle for you that will not result in continued learning. You need to know how to stimulate continued enthusiasm or when to admit defeat.

The saddest thing in my experience has been to see interested students who spent much time and effort, but learned very little because of inferior teaching methods. Their initial enthusiasm was lost to no purpose and their parents' lesson dollars were wasted. These casualties could have been prevented if the parents had known how to choose the right teacher.

A good beginning is crucial. If a student has already been given a poor beginning, only the highest quality instruction can correct the situation. There is no substitute for a first rate teacher. This book tells you what credentials are necessary and how to find such a teacher.

There are six absolute essentials for piano study, the absence of which will severely impair progress:

—A first rate teacher
—A good piano
—Interested parents
—A definite time schedule for practice
—A metronome
—A music dictionary

Learning to play piano is not instantaneous. If a child doesn't play beautifully in the beginning, a parent can become discouraged. Sometimes several years will pass with what seems like mediocre achievement before the rewards begin to show. Are you prepared to hang in there while this maturation occurs?

Most parents consider piano lessons an extra—not necessary, just nice. They don't expect their child to become a great artist or earn his living as a musician, they just hope he will learn a little about playing the piano. When your child enters first grade, do you think 'I don't care if he ever goes to college, I just want him to learn enough to get by.' Of course not. Whether it be piano lessons, or a college degree, build for the future.

Music is an essential ingredient in life. Piano lessons enrich the life of any child. Skills learned during piano studies enhance learning in other areas of a child's life. Hopefully this book will give parents the encouragement they need to start and keep their child on this exciting avenue of enjoyment. The benefits will indeed last a lifetime.

—*MARY TEEL JOHNSON*

NOTE: Obviously boys and girls are "he" and "she," but for ease of writing and reading, both sexes of students, parents and teachers will be referred to with the word "he" except in the case of specific examples.

PART I: THE STUDENT

CHAPTER 1

COMMON QUESTIONS ASKED BY PARENTS

WHAT IS THE RIGHT AGE TO START PIANO LESSONS?

In general, girls may start piano lessons at age seven, and boys at age eight. Girls seem to mature a bit faster than boys at this age, though the learning gap begins to even out around ages fifteen or sixteen. Then, many times, boys will surpass girls in academic subjects, as well as piano.

This opinion is necessarily a great simplification, since there are many exceptions, particularly with the gifted child. If indeed you have a young Mozart, your role in providing exceptional teaching must begin at an even earlier age. There are many bright and eager children who will be able to start piano at age five or six, if they have letter and number skills and love the piano.

Consider the vast amount of knowledge our children have before they start kindergarten. They have learned many language skills, as well as motor muscle skills. We've all taught our children nursery rhymes, jingles and phrases. At a very early age the child begins imitating sounds, often with little idea of what he is saying. To illustrate, how many adults can define a *tuffet* or *whey?*

Today, more than ever, young children have acquired enormous amounts of advanced information from television. They have a huge storehouse of sophisticated language and are quite knowledgeable about many subjects — even before they ever start learning to read.

At the age of seven or eight, the child has adequate motor and communications skills to be able to learn piano. He has learned to recognize the letters of the alphabet and learned both the look and value of numbers — skills necessary to the reading and learning of music. Also, by this age, most children have attended enough school to have at least a small amount of discipline, a limited attention span, and a slight understanding of the learning process.

Study of piano demands mind, eye, finger and hand coordination, plus the aural ability of hearing high or low sounds accurately. In addition, it requires the specialized discipline of using certain small

3

muscles that must be developed enough for them to control movement on the keyboard.

Boys need to be well started by the age of eight or nine, or very soon their natural interest in sports will interfere. This will make it increasingly difficult to get them started and keep them going.

Even at an early age, children are realists and they want to see results for their efforts. Piano lessons that do not teach them how to play something they can perform proudly, will make them easily and understandably discouraged. Proper teaching should have the child successfully performing pieces within the first year or he will start looking for excuses to quit.

A parent can accurately judge the readiness of his child by observing coordination and learning ability. If you are convinced he can benefit from lessons, by all means begin immediately.

WHAT TIME OF YEAR SHOULD PIANO LESSONS BEGIN?

The ideal time to begin young students in piano lessons is summertime. A few weeks after school gets out for the summer, children start to get bored and welcome new activities.

Most teachers expect students to study at least a semester. Consequently, vacancies in a teacher's schedule will be available in the summer, and again possibly at Christmas vacation time. Thus, these are the best times to arrange meetings with potential teachers.

To be accepted in the studio of a qualified piano teacher, you often must make inquiries and interviews at least a month in advance. Good teachers generally organize a fall schedule two or three months in advance, and often have their schedules full if you wait to call in September.

The advantage of starting in summer is that it allows the child to approach a new subject without other demands on his learning abilities. A short course in class piano lessons or private lessons at this time will give a teacher, parent and child a good idea of whether he is ready for piano lessons. During this initial exposure, his interest, mind-eye-hand coordination, attention span, and memory facility will be apparent.

The trial lessons should ideally be twice a week. Children forget quickly and need reinforcement. Only the teacher should instruct the child at this stage; attempts by parents to usurp the teacher's role can only be disastrous. Rarely can a parent assume dual roles of parent and teacher without creating confusion and perhaps hostility on the part of the child.

If the child is learning and enjoying the experience, by all means continue. However, if he is having problems or seems disinterested, do not despair. After three or six months, try again. Since individuals develop at such varying rates, especially in the arts, he might not be quite ready. Waiting until he is ready, will greatly increase his chance of success.

ARE SOME CHILDREN UNABLE TO LEARN PIANO?

The answer to this is a hestitant and qualified "yes." Although extremely rare, it is usually due to the presence of other learning difficulties, either mental or physical. Children with poor motor muscle control, or who lack manual dexterity will have problems. So will a child who suffers from dyslexia or reading difficulties.

In all my years of teaching, I have never encountered a totally impossible situation. I have taught children with very poor muscle control, and those who were slow to comprehend. I have even taught those who were slightly retarded, with encouraging results.

Most third grade children with average intelligence and ability can learn to play the piano — to a degree. Talent is a very scarce commodity. All children who take piano lessons will not develop into brilliant pianists, nor even into moderately good ones. They will, however, learn how to read music, count, and enjoy making pleasant sounds come out of a piano. In the beginning, piano lessons are just another mechanical skill.

Some people who are mentally very bright do not have manual dexterity. They are capable of achieving brilliant results in other fields, but the ability to make truly beautiful piano music is sadly lacking. Talent and musicianship, an innate ability and facility for music, occurs only in a small percentage of piano students. The extent to which these qualities are found in the child frequently determines the extent of his success at the piano.

At a more advanced stage, students will gain different benefits than the beginner, learning the various types of music, structure of compositions, styles of individual composers, and the discipline of learning complex music. To progress to this stage, more is required of a child, but in the beginning, the qualities discussed above will enable the child to test his potential.

After the first six weeks of lessons, any teacher worth his fee will give you a report on your child's progress. You and the teacher can assess the progress or lack of it, and decide on the course of action which is best for the child. *The child should not be present at such a meeting.*

I have known parents who were told by a qualified pianist and teacher that their child was without ability, who still wanted the child to study piano. They reasoned that the child would thereby improve his coordination, understand the printed page of music, and/or gain some self-confidence through learning a subject which was difficult for him. A decision of this kind is quite personal, and only honest expectations on both sides can produce satisfactory results.

CHAPTER 2
WHAT ABOUT TALENT?

WHAT IS THIS MYSTERIOUS THING CALLED TALENT?

By definition, talent is a "special natural ability or aptitude; a potentiality for achievement."

The word 'talent' is tossed about rather casually, and unfortunately both a parent and a student may receive a totally false notion of a child's real ability. Most private piano teachers use the word 'talent' too freely. Every parent wants to be told their child is talented.

With any piano student, some degree of talent or aptitude must exist. Coordination, comprehension of tonal sounds, ability to understand a musical line, a good memory, and a desire to play the piano must be present. Manual dexterity and a quick mind may masquerade as musical talent in a young child.

Real talent is not a common thing. Sometimes a certain degree of it exists, and this can be of great benefit to a child's musical studies. But that magic quality that makes the *great* pianist happens only rarely.

DOES MY CHILD HAVE IT?

How do you determine whether a child has *some* musical talent or *great* talent for piano? The child with exceptional musical gifts will have exhibited a great interest in 'finding' melodies on the keyboard, and will have shown an ability to do some astonishing things on the piano, even before he has had formal lessons. The child will comprehend and execute information rapidly. He will be thirsting for additional knowledge and assignments.

The very talented child will have shown his great interest in music at a very early age, usually by the time he is four years old. He will be spending a great deal of time at the piano, familiarizing himself with the instrument, and in many cases, will be able to play familiar melodies with no instruction. Piano will be an obvious and compelling part of the child's life.

The evaluation and training of a child who has great talent is a critical first step. In such rare circumstances, the average qualified teacher may not be capable of developing this special talent. The child will require an outstanding teacher, who is capable of guiding his progress and development.

If a parent has such a child, the parent should make an appointment at the nearest university or conservatory, and have the child evaluated by the best pianist-teacher available. Do not let the child continue to "play by ear" as the shift to note-reading music becomes more difficult every day.

THE "NATURAL" PIANIST

Some parents believe their child is a genius, and of course, they might be right. It will be a rare situation, as genius in any field is scarce. If your child has extraordinary capabilities, it will be quite evident to a good teacher.

If your child has shown a great interest in piano, and has taught himself to play several melodies by ear, he definitely needs a good teacher. Playing by ear is fun for the child and you, but he must learn the basic rudiments of reading, technique and form of compositions.

A good sense of rhythm is wonderful to find in a child. However, it will not explain the complicated rhythms of Haydn, Beethoven or Prokofiev. Native talent will accelerate your child's progress, but without instruction, native talent can be wasted.

At an audition/interview, do not spend your time, or the prospective teacher's, extolling your child's natural sense of rhythm or perfect pitch. Dwelling on the talent of a relative who could "play anything and never had a lesson in his life" will not make for a successful interview. If you want your child to learn the great literature of the piano, he must be taught. The longer he goes without lessons, the harder it becomes to introduce specific information that will make long-term progress successful.

THE GIFTED CHILD

Great talent and genius are closely related. They require special handling, and the sooner the better. It usually demands effort and expense on the part of the parent.

If his ability is corroborated by an expert, the child should be enrolled with an advanced teacher immediately. The fact that he is not with his own age group will have no bearing on his advancement or self-image. He will be like a dry sponge, eagerly absorbing every drop of information, and will spend countless hours at the piano, perfecting his instruction.

Most of our great performers were mature concert artists at least by the time they were sixteen years old. Many great pianists started their performance careers by ages seven to nine years. Many academic and music teachers may attempt to hold such a child back, pointing out that "he is too young," and that he should grow up socially with his peers, and other such general arguments. For the truly *great* talent, this is not true. That talent must be instructed and nurtured at the very beginning. When the precocious six year old is achieving what others might attain by their teens, he must be given excellent training immediately.

Superior instruction is first and foremost. However, many times it is a financial necessity to have a sponsor or to receive scholarship aid to continue piano study. Becoming an established concert pianist requires financial support. It takes money to provide fine teachers, a fine instrument, living, clothing and travel expenses. Great talent usually needs at least *some* good fortune. Being in the right place at the right time, and having the right people hear him perform is a fortunate thing. Cream certainly rises to the top, but the performer and his parents must live, as well.

GOOD, BUT NOT GREAT?

Since so very few people possess huge talent, what about those pianists who are very good, but may not achieve fame? Society needs these talented pianists desperately. There *must* be outstanding pianist/teachers in our universities and conservatories.

The decision to give a child, who manifests some talent, fine instruction should not be made on the basis that he will be a performing pianist. A parent must recognize that even a highly gifted child, given the finest instruction in piano, may still never become a great concert pianist. Many factors affect this ultimate goal for the big talent.

9

Although it is rare in the music world, there are 'slow starters' in piano as well as other fields. Paderewski was such a pianist. He played very well as a child, but did not plunge into the full-time concentration of becoming a concert pianist until he was nearly 22 years old. The teachers he went to at that time wrung their hands and told him "You are too old!" His marvelous talent and sheer willpower pushed those opinions aside, and his name became synonymous with a great pianist. It is quite possible that in today's world he might not have succeeded. His playing, in the grand romantic style, was very much in vogue during his lifetime, and he possessed that magical panache that comes across the footlights. He was essentially a careless pianist, with many technical short-comings, according to the technique-perfect standards of today. But his talent and personality were so great that despite the many deficiencies in his playing, he captured the audiences of the world with his fleet fingers, luxuriant red hair, and magnificent stage presence.

CHILD PRODIGIES

Paderewski's career is not average, by any means. The majority of child prodigies become famous at a much earlier age. Artur Rubenstein and Josef Hofmann made their concert debuts at age seven!

Although a splendid pianist, Horowitz was not a child prodigy, but did make his Russian debut as a pianist when he was sixteen years old. It was not until he was nearly 24, that he came to the United States to electrify audiences with his exciting approach to the keyboard.

Great talent *must* be present for a potential artist-pianist to succeed, but there are many other factors that enter into the development of a career as a concert pianist. Many of our great artists have had an "angel" who helped support them during the creation of their piano performance careers. Occasionally an established performer will exhibit an interest in the career of a young pianist.

Sometimes, potential artists are forced to work at other jobs, while trying to get started. The lives of many of our great pianists are filled with stories of horrendous difficulties in staying alive. Rubenstein found himself "borrowing" money from friends, and was a frequent "house guest" of those who recognized his enormous pianistic ability. Rachmaninoff wanted only to compose music, and not perform as a pianist. However, as a refugee from the Russian revolution, he found it necessary to concertize to support himself, his wife and two small daughters. The musical community of the United States gave him, and many others, assistance and support. Very few of our great performers, past or present, have had an easy time establishing their careers.

Paderewski is credited with saying that his piano playing was "99 percent perspiration, and 1 percent inspiration." That statement is open for discussion. Regardless, *great* talent must exist to make a great concert pianist.

CHAPTER 3
WHAT IS REQUIRED OF PARENTS?

GIVING YOUR SUPPORT

Piano lessons for your child require something of you, the parent or guardian. Just delivering a child to a lesson and picking him up afterwards, is not enough. There must be some support for a child of any age. Support does not mean hovering around the piano when the child is trying to practice. It does not mean stepping into the role of the teacher.

Support means your encouragement and love. At the very beginning, with the very young child, sometimes it means just sitting with him at the piano while he goes over his finger drills and pieces. Practicing is a lonely business and young children can feel isolated until they learn to enjoy their practice time alone.

Patience is very difficult for a parent to give to his own child. How much easier it is to be patient with other people's children! If a child is told to "practice softly" or "do it later" because Dad has his favorite program to watch on TV, this can kill any desire by the child to practice and progress.

You must remember that you are still the most important person in your child's life. Your encouragement and tact are going to mean a great deal, and probably will be an important factor as to whether or not your child will succeed.

THE HOME SCHEDULE

Your home schedule must accommodate itself to the necessity for a definite time of quiet and availability of the piano for your child. No one can succeed in learning anything if there is a constant running through the house by other children, noises, or shouted orders from the parent to "do it again."

Home schedules must be arranged so that you give your child a chance for achievement. Arranging household activities so that the student can have that quiet, available time is not only necessary for the child's learning, but also for both of you to get your money's worth from a lesson.

PARENTS AT LESSONS

Parents should be welcome at a lesson — but not every time. The young, beginning student may need the parent at the first two or three lessons. It's frightening to go into a stranger's home or studio and not have the back-up of a parent. New material and new surroundings are difficult for the little ones to endure. After a month of lessons, at the most, encourage the child to attend the lesson alone. More will be accomplished.

When a parent is in the room during the lesson, a child has a great difficulty deciding whom to please — mommy or teacher. If Johnny makes a mistake, and a parent instantly interjects "He played it perfectly at home," there is a problem. Parents should remain silent during a lesson, unless there is a glaring omission of explanation. Even then, it is far better to clarify it at another time. A parent's apology, or request for information at a lesson undermines the student's trust in a teacher.

With the teenage student, I think it is wonderful if a parent wishes to attend an occasional lesson. It allows them to observe the teaching process, to see how well or badly the student reacts. Questions or doubts should be expressed privately. I believe the teenage student, in many ways, needs the active support of a parent more than the very young because he is less sure of himself.

Whether at the lesson, or at home, do not try to take over the teacher's role. Children establish a rapport with their teachers and have a special relationship with them, something that is healthy for their emotional growth. Parents should respect this. Let the teacher instruct, as you continue to give your support.

OVER-SCHEDULING A CHILD

If you want successful piano lessons, do not schedule your child's time with too many other activities. A child can manage school, an outside activity such as Brownies, Scouts or a sport, and still study piano. Going beyond that and involving the child in ice-skating, ballet, horse-back riding or other time and energy consuming activities, puts an impossible drain on his time.

With too many activities, a child usually will excel at none, and may feel defeated in his effort to please you. Youth is a very brief time of life. Much can be accomplished by a young person, but only within reasonable bounds. There are a limited number of hours in a day, and filling every second produces a schedule that would exhaust an Olympic athlete

The absolute minimum amount of practice time necessary for a piano student is an hour a day, every day. For the capable and serious piano student, the time must be increased to two hours or more a day. If both parent and child want piano lessons, help arrange his life so he may succeed and still have the pleasures of childhood.

CHAPTER 4
FRINGE BENEFITS

MORE THAN MUSIC

Because of its completeness, the study of piano is a must for all musicians even though their major instrument may be violin, clarinet or whatever. All conservatory and university trained musicians are required to complete several courses of piano study. Though this will not make them proficient enough to perform as piano soloists, it will give them the ability to comprehend the variety of sound in a complete orchestration.

It is of great importance that parents of children who wish to study any instrument have the child taught to read piano music and acquire some keyboard facility. The student may opt to spend the majority of his time on another instrument. However, he will have this basic knowledge of piano to assist both his own studies and those he may someday teach.

Obversely, the dedicated piano student should have lessons in at least one other orchestral intrument to give him a comprehension of the group aspect of music, called ensemble playing. This knowledge will enhance his ability to perform with an orchestra, accompany, or be part of a trio or quartet.

I have always thought that the fringe benefits from a good musical education are *almost* equal to the ability to play great piano music. While a few students will continue studying piano through college or conservatory, and will choose piano teaching or performance as a career, *all* students have added a beautiful dimension to their lives. Despite the fact that our educational system does not acknowledge the importance of music other than for school bands and orchestras, there are many wonderful things that occur as a result of studying piano.

There follows a list of some of these wonderful benefits:

COORDINATION

The study of piano employs the mind, the eyes, the individual fingers, the feet, and the entire body. While learning the joy of sound, the student is reinforcing the skills of coordination. This kind of coordination is necessary for driving a car, shop skills, sports, dancing and typing, to name a few of many activities.

ORGANIZATION OF MATERIAL TO BE LEARNED

In order to achieve mastery over a solo or study, the material must be thoroughly understood and organized in the mind. If a student learns how to do this with piano music, the skill can easily be applied to the study of chemistry, language, engineering or creative writing.

CONCENTRATION

It is completely impossible to learn to play the piano without concentrating on what the mind and eye are telling the fingers to do. The ability to keep one's concentration while performing an intricate and difficult piece of music is a learned technique. This skill is usable in hundreds of ways throughout life.

Some may wonder why concentration and a quiet audience are so important to a fine piano performance. All of us have enjoyed background music by a pianist in a fine restaurant or other social situations. This type of quasi-improvisational piano playing generally consists of popular music with simple melodies and limited chord changes. Mistakes can be easily disguised by adjustments to chord or melodic line, flourishes or modulation into another piece of music.

It is doubtful if pianists such as Eddie Duchin, Carmen Cavallero, Roger Williams or Art Tatum ever played a piece the same way twice. Their dexterity of mind and fingers, and knowledge of chords and key signatures, allowed them to superimpose their style over the generally unsophisticated harmony and melody. Performers of this type are rare, very good, and endowed with a native talent for improvisation.

Performing a complex, classical piece of music, with special notes, rhythms and melody lines, requires accurate reproduction by the pianist. Hence, proper learning and memorizing, combined with intense concentration is necessary for successful performance. Occasionally great pianists make mistakes during a concert which they cover well enough so that non-musicians will not hear them. This is more easily done in Romantic, Impressionistic and Contemporary piano literature. Even the non-musician will hear a mistake made in a piece by Bach, Scarlatti, Mozart or Beethoven. These compositions are so well constructed and precise that an error cannot be covered by a trill or insertion of other notes.

POISE

Learning to get up in front of other people and perform all alone is a fantastic capability. In every field, there are many people who are exceptionally bright and competent, and as such make excellent employees. But if that person is unable to keep his poise in meetings and job-related situations where it is necessary to stand up in front of a group and discuss information, he will lose out to someone who may not be quite as brilliant, but who can keep his presence of mind.

MEMORY TRAINING

The memory training achieved by taking piano lessons is an advantage in all phases of life. Anyone in any business knows how important it is to remember names, telephone numbers and details concerning transactions with others. Many very successful executives will readily admit that a good memory can masquerade as brilliance in many situations.

It is an educational loss that schools no longer require a large amount of memorization as in former times. The concept that a child should not be required to memorize facts, poems or speeches is new to education. Currently it is considered better for children to discover facts for themselves, rather than learning them by rote. This is good only if the child has enough information to attempt discovery alone.

Young children memorize vast amounts of information, not the least of which is their spoken language. A small percentage of people have astounding memories, often called *photographic* memories. Average people can learn and strengthen memory skills if properly taught. The memorizing required by a study of piano can be a valuable exercise, benefitting all other areas of education.

Types of memory: We must distinguish between physical and mental memory. All of us have learned an incredible amount of

17

physical memory by age four — how to hold a spoon, fork, cup, turn a door handle, lift a toy, climb on a chair or open a drawer. These are all *physical* memories. We do not have to rethink them each time we repeat them. This kind of muscular memory, referred to as *kinetic memory*, relates to our activities in everyday life. (Instinct, on the other hand, is the body's reaction to danger by removing the hand from a hot surface or dodging a falling object.)

Kinetic memory in music is an essential part of learning a solo. The muscles of the fingers must go over a certain pattern many times until the muscles are trained to go to specific notes on the keyboard. Depending solely on this kind of physical memory can be insufficient in a concert if there is a distraction that interrupts the *thread* of the performance. The *intellectual memory* must constantly direct the fingers — the mind must know the plan of the piece, key signature, where it starts and ends — to navigate the complicated labyrinth of a complete solo.

An example of how the kinetic and intellectual memories work together is seen in the performance of a great pianist. Before beginning to play, he will sit quietly at the piano. This is not a pose, but is the preparation of the mind to perform what it has learned.

Many concert artists will play entire programs with their eyes closed. They are mentally reading the music from the page. This mental imagery is an essential part of intellectual memory. Every student should be encouraged to close his eyes and "see" the solo in front of him.

There are many areas of learning that require analyzing, investigative thinking and personal curiosity. Inventors, composers, or anyone doing highly original creative work, must have far more in his mind than just memory tools. In any event, the vast majority of individuals will be more successful in whatever their field with a well trained memory.

SENSE OF ACHIEVEMENT AND CHARACTER DEVELOPMENT

Piano lessons are a great character builder. The piano student finds that he can really *do* something that most others can't. He finds he can perform under pressure and shine above others. Even the shyest person will start developing people skills when he finds he is successful at the piano. The admiration of his peers can literally change his life. It follows that this ability to play the piano makes a person more popular all his life. He is sought after both in and out of school. As an adult, he can move easily from one community to another, and through his musical skill make instant friendships. The individual with musical ability will always stand out from the crowd.

The student who has learned, memorized and performed in public, as well as he can at that particular time, enjoys a sense of self-achievement that is tremendous! He *did* it! He *can do* it! He has had the opportunity to prove himself in a situation of stress. He can perform *all alone.* That accomplishment can, and does, affect his whole attitude toward himself, all his life.

PART II: THE TEACHER

CHAPTER 5
THE RIGHT PIANO TEACHER

"There is this nice little old lady, right down the street . . ."

"Oh, I don't PLAY the piano anymore, I just TEACH."

"My neighbor has this teacher who comes right to her house."

"I believe the minister's wife 'gives' piano lessons."

"But do you teach Theory?"

WHY CREDENTIALS ARE IMPORTANT

The majority of parents do not know how or where to start to find a piano teacher for their child. Because this problem is so widespread, many of them do it wrong. They talk to a neighbor whose child is studying piano and go to that teacher without further research. Or they go to that "nice little old lady down the street" who "gives" piano lessons (as though a quality lesson could be given away for nothing), or the minister's wife because she plays piano for Sunday school.

Now, if any of these people also have proper credentials and compatible personalities, your search is over. What concerns me is that often these people have assumed a role for which they are not trained or qualified. They often have this role thrust upon them by a community based simply on the fact that they can play a few notes on a piano and that other teachers are unavailable.

You and your child will be embarking on a learning experience that can be a joy for a lifetime. It may be the foundation for the child's college education, and it might turn into his profession. Whatever the ultimate result, the beginning is the *most* important time. If you build a house, the first consideration is a good solid foundation. If you slight on that, it really doesn't matter how lovely the wall-to-wall carpet is, or how large the closets are. You have put an expensive home on a poor foundation.

I cannot stress enough the importance of superb teaching at the beginning. It is sad to note that the average piano student usually has the first few years of piano lessons wasted by unqualified and uninspired teaching. It is amazing that such a child can later desire to continue lessons at all! If you are in this situation, it is too late to start at the beginning again, but you must correct the situation immediately.

DIFFERENT TEACHERS FOR DIFFERENT AGE LEVELS

The parent must know what kind of teacher he is trying to find. There are teachers who prefer working with the younger child, and there are those who prefer the older student. Those who teach predominately younger children have geared their studio and approach to that age group. Likewise there are teachers who prefer to work with more mature children.

The wonderful beginning teacher may not be satisfactory for the teenage student. That student may feel out of place in a studio of mainly young pupils. Usually you do not want to place your seven-year-old in a studio of advanced performers. He will always feel he is the worst, will play first in any program, and will play the least difficult solo. The teenage student in a younger group will always play last on any program, and the most difficult piece, still feeling out of place. Consequently, a parent should endeavor to investigate the type of studio a teacher has, before scheduling an audition/interview.

Most education systems separate students on the basis of age or competency. A college professor is not particularly good at teaching fourth grade, nor is a kindergarten teacher capable of teaching at college level. The same holds true with piano teaching.

NECESSARY QUALIFICATIONS

1. A university degree in piano performance, piano pedagogy (profession of teaching), a public school music degree with a major in piano, or a conservatory degree.
2. Membership in the State Music Teachers Association.
3. Membership in the Music Teachers National Association.
4. Regularly scheduled studio performance classes, and at least one yearly recital.
5. A studio location and good piano, whether in a home or business location.

Now I am well aware that a degree does not necessarily make a marvelous teacher. There are many people who have excellent credentials, but do not relate well to others. However, a parent must have a starting point for beginning the selection process. Proper credentials have to be number one on the list.

The good teacher should belong to the State Music Teachers Association, which is in turn part of the Music Teachers National Association (MTNA). That organization has made substantial gains in raising the credentials of piano teachers in each state. Members receive a quarterly magazine that contains new materials, information on various teaching methods, articles by master teachers and reports of activities from all over the United States. The MTNA also publishes a national directory of member-teachers in all 50 states, as an assistance to students who are moving to another state.

Each state has its own method of rating teachers. Many states will have three categories: first, one for those with master's degrees or more; second, one for those with bachelor's degrees; and third, one for non-degreed teachers. It is important to know which category your teacher is in. While membership does not assure special competence, it does indicate the teacher's special training. When questioned about credentials, teachers should not become defensive. Well-trained teachers welcome the opportunity to discuss their training and expertise.

The national and state music teachers associations are making a great effort to upgrade the quality of piano teaching. The quality and procedure of state music contests are in accordance with the aims and suggestions of the MTNA to produce competent students.

Since there are no laws which prevent anyone from opening a piano studio, it is necessary for the parent to make all these inquiries about credentials and experience.

THE NON-DEGREED TEACHER

The day of the non-degreed teacher is essentially past. Most state music organizations had to begin their associations with "grandfather" clauses because many of the older teachers did not have degrees. Now, all conservatories, colleges and universities demand a degree from all members of their faculties. Usually, these teachers must have at least a master's degree in their chosen field. Degrees and credentials represent ability combined with many years of work and expense.

The longer I taught, the more I became convinced that great teachers are *born* not made. Some individuals seem to have that magic quality that makes them fine instructors. Even so, a course of formal study and training, accompanied by requisite degrees and credentials, will serve to elevate those individuals to a position of prominence.

THE NON-PERFORMING TEACHER

Do not assume that teachers who no longer perform in public concerts are not good teachers. They must have credentials, and knowledge of what they teach. But many fine musicians are just not performers. Sometimes it is because they started piano later in life, and sometimes it is due to their personal nervous systems, which will not take the stress of walking out on a stage.

They *should* have had to perform at least a few times in college, or they could not have passed their piano "juries", where performance is required. For many pianist-teachers, those will be the last times they perform in public, and they will devote their skills to teaching. Ideally, a teacher will continue some performance throughout his career, but many do not.

On the other end, many of our great pianist performers do not care to teach. Their talent is in performance, and not in teaching. Performers and teachers are not always cut out of the same cloth. Ordinarily you will find that wonderful combination of performance and pedagogy more easily at a university or conservatory, where a performing faculty is both desired and necessary. Since performers must spend many hours every day, maintaining and enlarging their repertoire, plus the performances themselves, it frequently becomes impossible to combine both performing and teaching careers.

TEACHERS THAT DON'T QUALIFY

There are enormous numbers of teachers who will not meet your requirements. These generally are teachers who are chosen for reasons of convenience, rather than credentials. If a teacher with fine credentials happens to fit in these categories, that is another matter, but never choose a teacher based solely on the reasons listed below:

1. The teacher is a convenient neighbor or friend. It is never wise to choose on the basis of friendship or geography, even though it might be easier for parents to get the child to lessons.

2. The teacher makes house calls. Again, it may be enormously convenient to have a teacher come to your home, but if a teacher has time to do this, you can rest assured he is not top quality. If he were, he would have a studio location and his time would be too valuable to drive to homes of individual students.

3. The teacher does not belong to the State Music Teachers Association.

4. The teacher makes an idol out of theory. Good teachers teach theory at every lesson with scales, arpeggios, cadences, triads, chord positions, key signatures and time signatures. Your child will receive all the theory he needs as he progresses until he is quite proficient at the piano and actually plays well. If he intends to study piano at university level, the first quarter or semester of Theory 1 will cover any exotic points he might have missed up to that time.

5. The teacher relies on more written work than keyboard experience.

WHEN IT'S TIME TO CHANGE TEACHERS

Because of the varying requirements of a student at different levels in his studies, a change of teachers during the child's piano education is not unusual. A good teacher will tell you when he thinks a change could be beneficial. His studio may not be geared to working with all ages, any more than the one-room schoolhouse could be compared to our educational system of today.

If the teacher does not mention this imminent change, then the parent must. Many times, parents will feel embarrassed to broach the subject of a change. They have trusted and respected this fine teacher for several years, and possibly have become personal friends. They may feel obligated to continue forever with the beginning teacher.

This is poor reasoning. Many of these highly qualified beginning teachers never intended to teach advanced students. If their degree is in music education and they studied piano as an elective subject, it is highly possible that they did not have the time nor ability to learn the advanced literature of the keyboard. One must remember that no teacher can teach what he does not know. As in *The Music Man*, "ya gotta know the territory."

In rare instances, you will find the gifted teacher who can take a student from learning middle C right through the Beethoven sonatas and Chopin etudes. Since this usually is not the case, a parent must be aware that piano teachers specialize, just as other educators do. Selecting the right teacher for your student is a difficult task.

CHAPTER 6
The Search For The Right Teacher

HOW TO BEGIN

The attitude of many parents is "We'll get Susie started on piano, and if she shows any promise or interest, *then* we will go to a better teacher." If you start with the less competent teacher, when you finally decide to change to a qualified one, much harm has been done already. Much of what has been taught must be *un*taught. You have wasted precious time in your child's life, dulled the initial enthusiasm for piano lessons, and spent money on a product that is not worth the investment.

I cannot stress enough the importance of superb teaching at the *beginning*. It is sad to note that the average piano student usually has the first one-to-three years of piano lessons wasted by inept, unqualified and uninspired teaching. Many parents have this problem and are endeavoring to correct the situation. They cannot start over at the beginning, but must start where they are at the present time.

Here are some steps towards a successful search:

1. Contact the local store, or stores, that sell pianos. Usually they will have a list of piano teachers in the area.
2. Contact the music department of any university, college, or junior college near you. They will know of the qualified piano teachers.
3. Contact the professional music organizations in your area. Look in the Yellow Pages under "Music Teachers" or "Piano Teachers." Usually there will be a listing for the State Music Teaching organization. They have lists of teachers, and information about them.
4. Contact the professional music organizations that present concerts in your area. They will know of the local musicians and their reputations.

Now you have quite a few names in front of you. Start calling on the telephone. Do not call in the afternoon, since private piano teachers are teaching at that time. The hours when they can teach are normally limited to after school, Saturdays, Sundays or evenings. If they are teaching, ask them to return your call. Here are some questions to ask:

"Do you have a degree in piano, or music education?"

"Could you tell me something about your piano teaching experience?"

"Do you perform? Have you ever performed?"

"Where did you receive your musical training?"

"In what age-group are the majority of the students in your studio?"

"Do you have recitals? May I attend one?"

"What do you charge? Is payment in advance, by statement, monthly or quarterly?"

"Do you belong to the State Music Teachers Association?"

From your telephone information, contact three teachers who are possible choices for your purposes. Make an appointment to see each at his convenience. Take your child with you. Expect to pay for the appointment. Usually an hour is necessary. If the teacher did not mention a fee, you should ask the charge for an audition/interview. Do not expect to use an hour of a teacher's time and receive information without paying for it.

After you have kept, and paid for, two or three appointments, both you and your child have formed some opinions. The child may be drawn more to one teacher than another. If the qualifications are good for all of them, and if you've done your homework they should be, *listen* to your child's preference. A private lesson is a very intimate learning experience. There must be good rapport between student and teacher. The association may last several years, and be of great influence on your child. It must be a good, working relationship.

Hopefully, you will be able to sense that special quality that marks the "born" teacher" when you have an interview with a potential piano teacher. Listening to your child's opinion is a very good idea. Children have an uncanny way of determining if a person really likes young people and enjoys teaching.

THE VALUE AND COST OF A FINE TEACHER

If you follow the suggestions given for finding that right piano teacher, you will be making a decision and selection of great consequence. The opinions of a private teacher may well determine how your child thinks about many subjects besides piano. The private teacher should possess not only the necessary musical knowledge, but also share some of your ideas on behavior, morality and integrity. If the relationship continues over a period of years, that private teacher will be a role model for your child.

That's a pretty big order, isn't it? A professional who meets all those requirements is rare. Sometimes he is not always nearby. Usually he will be expensive.

The area of piano teaching seems to be very murky in many people's minds. The public seems to think that because someone loves piano music, and is teaching young people, that earning money is secondary to them. What an insult! Piano teachers have studios to maintain, homes, grocery bills and living expenses just like any other professional. A teacher cannot live on the love of music alone.

Consider the fees you pay a doctor, dentist, lawyer, or tax consultant and the fees you pay the hairdresser, plumber, or carpenter. Today, many service people charge as much as many professional people. Of course service people have achieved expertise through their work or vocational school, rather than through university or college education. A well-qualified piano teacher has completed both schooling and teaching experience. Expect to pay an hourly wage that is comparable to that charged by other professional or service people.

Fewer and fewer conservatory and university piano graduates who *want* to teach private piano lessons can afford to do so. They must affiliate with a music school or try to get a position in a public or private school The entire nature of private piano teaching below college level is changing in America. Schools of music are becoming more common. A number of private piano teachers join together in an effort to pursue their careers and still make a living. Do investigate such schools carefully. Some are excellent, some are not.

I believe that the music school approach is the wave of the future, as the private studio often is not a financial success. Whether your search results in an individual studio situation or a music school, go through the same process of calling, paying for an audition/interview, and choosing the best there is for your child.

Regardless of whether the child ever uses his piano skills to earn his living, or has them as a life enhancement, you will have spent your money wisely on his development by choosing the right teacher.

FINDING QUALIFIED TEACHERS IN RURAL AREAS

If you happen to have a gifted, credentialed pianist-teacher in a small town or remote area, you are extremely fortunate. It seems to occur rarely. The suggestions of inquiring for piano teachers at large music stores, colleges and universities can be quite difficult for you to do. There may be only one teacher, or none, in your area, and you do not have the choices available to urban dwellers.

You should follow the same steps in the larger city or town nearest you. If at all possible, try to join forces with other parents in your town who also want a qualified piano teacher. Then, perhaps at considerable inconvenience and expense, keep two or three appointments with potential teachers to determine if they measure up to what you require.

If you find a qualified teacher, take turns driving three or four children to the city for their private piano lessons once a week. Many great talents have come from small towns dotted across our country and they have achieved their musical training in just this way. It takes a much greater effort on your part to find proper instruction and get your child to his lessons regularly than for city dwellers, but even if you have to do it alone, the effort is easily justified by the results.

Another possible option would be to locate a piano teacher or a master piano student at the college or universtiy nearest your rural area. If there is assurance that the teacher can fill a day with students, sometimes you can have him come to your community one day a week.

This option requires the cooperation of a public school, so that students may be excused for 45 minutes or an hour, in order to take the private lesson. Many times, the school is willing to accommodate such a situation, if the piano teacher has credentials acceptable to school standards.

When I opened my first piano studio, I was in need of some assured income. A neighboring community desperately wanted a well-qualified piano teacher. The parents arranged with the school system a plan where I could spend an entire day teaching the students in this small town. It worked out very well for all concerned. Since the school was near the location available for private piano lessons, students were absent from school class rooms a minimum amount of time, and yet were able to receive good piano training from a degreed teacher.

The small community that is some distance from a larger city usually does not have many choices of private teachers. It is not always easy to find a solution. However, I encourage you to try. If you have a talented, interested child, he is worth the effort. Many fine talents could be lost to us if such a child is taught by a teacher with little expertise. Remember those early years are the golden ones, where the foundation for future study is laid.

CHAPTER 7
AUDITIONS AND INTERVIEWS

"I don't want my son to be a concert pianist . . ."

"I just want Joan to be able to play for her own enjoyment."

"Does he really have to play scales?"

"Susan likes to write her own music . . ."

"He figured out the Moonlight Sonata all by himself."

WHAT ARE THEY, AND ARE THEY NECESSARY?

An audition/interview is a necessary step in the selection of a teacher. This initial meeting serves three functions: 1) the teacher can find out what the student knows, 2) the parent can see how that teacher goes about teaching and interacting with the student, and 3) the personalities of all parties concerned, by interacting, can gauge how the working relationship will be.

At the audition/interview, let the teacher and the child do the talking. The teacher does not want to hear from the parent that the child is talented or quick or capable of picking out "little tunes by himself," or even that he can write his own music. The parent should remain silent unless questioned by the teacher, and should not answer for the child or put words into his mouth.

Teachers ordinarily like to ask questions such as: "Do you like to play the piano?" "What kind of piece did you like best?" "Did your former teacher have you work on finger drills and scales?" A new teacher will also want to hear the child play something, both to watch his approach to playing, as well as his ability and technique. Sometimes this can be traumatic for the student, for unfortunately, there are children who have taken lessons for six months or even six years who sit in front of a keyboard and can play nothing.

VALUE OF FIRST IMPRESSIONS

First impressions are important. Everyone has met someone they did not particularly like at first, only to find that in time, they became good friends. However, far more often, if a first impression is negative on either the part of parent or child, they will not take the time to find out that "George is a great guy once you get to know him."

Something for a parent to notice in a good teacher is his ability to come up with something positive to say. No student should leave an interview feeling that the situation is completely hopeless, and that he should just forget about studying piano. It is unfortunate that there are some teachers who proceed in just this negative fashion, who try to destroy before they start building. This type of teaching most commonly appears with the very advanced pianist-teacher who is only concerned with producing artists, not trying to make someone enjoy playing the piano. In this case, compliments just muddy up the water as far as the teacher is concerned. Older students, sometimes, can accept this harsh approach if they are dedicated enough to believe in themselves and their own capabilities and know inside that they will eventually succeed. With young students or insecure teenagers, this negative, destroy-first approach should *never* be used.

Before the audition/interview ever takes place, the child should be reassured that the teacher does not expect a Carnegie Hall performance. Music may be used, mistakes may occur, but the main thrust of this meeting is to see if that teacher is the one you and your child can work with. Teacher, parent and student will find out what is expected and how the relationship will work musically, mentally and physically.

HOW TO MAKE A BAD IMPRESSION

Sometimes a child will volunteer to play an obviously impossible solo. Frequently this turns out to be a simplified version of the main theme of a piece, in which case both the parent and child have been cheated by a poor teacher into thinking they were playing a great piece of music. Simplified music is to great music what comic books are to Shakespeare. The use of simplified versions of great compositions is widespread, and in my opinion, very wrong. There is an ample supply of wonderful original compositions by the Masters that are simple enough for beginners and are far superior.

Another unfortunate occurrence is for an older student to slog through a difficult piece that they "have worked out themselves," with oceans of wrong notes and rhythms, and terrible technique. This will make a poor impression on a good teacher, who will suggest that the child begin on all new material. Forcing a child to relearn a piece he has already learned wrong is extremely difficult.

A third thing new teachers dislike is having a parent choose what the child is to be taught. Even if both you and your child are enchanted by a particular composition, the teacher has reasons for selecting certain solos and studies that he feels are best for the particular stage of development your child has achieved. This is entirely the province of an instructor, and the parent should respect this fact.

IF THE CHILD IS HAVING A BAD DAY

If your child is in a particularly rotten or sullen mood the day of the scheduled interview, keep the appointment anyway. A good teacher must be, in many ways, an amateur psychologist, being able to recognize that shyness or terse hostility in a child are signs of extreme nervousness. Hopefully, the new teacher will understand that both student and teacher are apt to feel defensive in such a situation, and knows how to relieve the tension in a way that will allow the child to smile and relax a bit.

Should the child not be able to play *something*, a solo or a scale, then the teacher should ask the child to sight-read some easy material. This will allow the teacher to see what the child knows of the printed page of music, and how his fingers react with his mind.

If the parent tells a teacher "Susan likes to write her own music," there is a definite problem. Composition and originality are marvelous and rare talents that should not be discouraged. But before creation can take place, there must be knowledge. We must assume that Shakespeare had an excellent comprehension of the written and spoken language *before* he started writing his plays and sonnets.

The audition/interview is worth both the time and money you spend on it. A telephone call simply will not suffice to make all the discoveries available in a personal meeting.

CHAPTER 8
A PROFESSIONAL RELATIONSHIP

WHAT IS IT?

What is professionalism? It is that character, spirit and method that distinguish a professional from an amateur. Your audition/interview will provide you with an opportunity to appraise a prospective teacher in this regard, both through conversation and observation.

The professional musician is earning his livelihood from his skill and maintains a schedule that encompassess time for lessons, performance classes and a yearly recital. He will have knowledge of and access to additional performance opportunities and entry to various contests. He will be more than willing to discuss all these things with you at your first meeting.

A professional expects to be treated as one. With no real intent on their part, many parents treat a private piano teacher with less respect than they would any other professional. Sometimes, this is partially a teacher's fault. If he does not have a high regard for himself and his studio, his behavior can foster this second-class-citizen treatment. Private teachers *may* become good friends, over a period of time, but at the lesson, it should be strictly business.

NO FIRST NAMES, PLEASE

If you know the teacher as a personal friend, you may be in the habit of using his first name. However, at a piano lesson, and in home discussions with your child, always refer to the teacher as Mr., Mrs. or Ms. so-and-so — *never* using first names. The child must know that the lesson is a special time and that the teacher is not a personal friend at that moment.

The unquestioned usage of first names by many people is meant to be friendly. However, it can result in an uncomfortable familiarity which can detract from the professionalism of the lesson arrangement. Personally I resent the use of my first name by doctors, nurses or attorneys who are strangers to me. Courtesy requires the use of whatever title a person possesses, until such time as permission to use a first name is granted. Set an example for your child by extending this courtesy and formality to the teacher.

THE STUDIO

The location, equipment and appearance of a studio will reveal a great deal about a prospective teacher. Many studios for young students are located in private homes. Some studios will be in a room made expressly for that purpose. Other studios may be located in a den that is used as a studio, or — horrors! — a roughed-in porch or unattractive basement.

A piano studio should be well lighted, clean and attractive. There should be an excellent piano; it is the teacher's most requisite equipment. Sometimes studios will have two pianos available. The studio should be equipped with a clock, a metronome, and possibly a tape recorder, so the student may hear his performance occasionally. The piano should be dusted, always in tune, with clean, washed keys. Since many pianists have perspiring fingers and hands, a not-uncommon nervous physical reaction, tissues should be available to wipe hands and keyboard.

A piano studio needs to have a bathroom available for students to use. If a child arrives at his piano lesson directly after school, he will need bathroom facilities. The bathroom should be supplied with paper or cloth towels, soap, toilet paper, tissues, a wide-toothed comb, and a waste basket.

DRESS AND DEPORTMENT

A good teacher will "dress for success." Because of his position as role model for the child, a professional teacher will always be well groomed. A teacher who conducts a lesson dressed in jeans or a jogging suit is not suitably attired. In any business office, dress codes demand a certain professionalism; so also in a private business. Because a person is in an artistic field, that does not give him license to be careless in these matters. Both your child and the teacher should attend a lesson in clean, tidy and suitable clothing.

LESSON APPOINTMENTS

With the limited time available to a private teacher for teaching lessons, the teacher must schedule his time closely. It is his obligation to stay on schedule with lesson appointments. Realistically, piano teachers make every effort to stay within ten minutes of a scheduled lesson time. Still, your child should be at his lesson at the scheduled time. If he arrives ten minutes late, it is impossible for the teacher to give him his full time without intruding on the following student's lesson.

Each piano teacher has his own procedure for handling missed lessons and should explain this at the first meeting. Most will try to make up a lesson the child has missed; a few teachers will not and will still expect payment for that time.

Most private piano teachers will endeavor to adjust lesson times when special situations interfere with the scheduled time. Sometimes it is possible for your child to change with another student to accommodate a play rehearsal or special occasion. While changes should not occur frequently, piano teachers do understand orthodontist appointments or a crisis. If there is a protracted illness, individual arrangements can be made with piano teachers. Family emergencies do arise where a student may have to miss several lessons. However, avoid asking for a change except when it is absolutely necessary, since a private teacher cannot keep changing a schedule for one student.

Courtesy and consideration demand that the piano teacher be given adequate notice when a lesson will be missed. If a teacher is not given sufficient notice, usually 24 hours, the teacher may feel no obligation to make up a missed lesson. Calling a few minutes before a scheduled lesson time is not enough notice, and you should expect to be charged for that lesson. Telephone calls are disruptive during teaching times and you should not usurp the lesson time of other students.

Remember not to burden the teacher with a long explanation of why the lesson was missed. If a teacher finds an alternate time for a make-up lesson, keep the apointment. He is doing you a courtesy in rescheduling. Respect this special consideration and make every attempt to abide by the teacher's schedule.

PAYMENTS

A piano lesson is an intangible. Once it is over, there is no proof it happened except in the student's mind. Many people have the mistaken idea that music teachers teach because they love piano so much. Indeed, they *do* love the piano and their teaching, but their monthly expenses come due as regularly as yours. If a studio is located in a private home, a parent may assume that a prompt payment is not critical, and may be made at the parent's convenience. This attitude is not only poor business, it is offensive.

Studios vary in their methods of payment. Some studios, particularly schools of music, will require a quarterly payment in advance. Most private piano studios require a month's payment in advance. If a studio mails statements at the end of the month, the payment should be returned by mail. Do *not* send a check, or cash, with a child to the lesson. It is demeaning to the teacher to be paid by a child. You, the parent, hired the teacher, and you should make the payment by mail or in person.

Here are some of the things you should avoid saying to a credentialed private piano teacher:

—"Gosh, I must have lost your statement."

—"But I was *sure* I sent a check with Diane."

—"I'll try to get caught up next month ... you know how it is."

—"Guess I just forgot ... hope you understand."

Your attention to the financial details of piano lessons are important to the relationship between the teacher, you and your child. Do not mar the relationship by late payments or forgetfulness. Whatever method is used by the teacher you choose, be prompt in payment.

Complete your payments to a former teacher before engaging a new one. No ethical teacher will accept a new student who still owes money to a former teacher. It is wrong of a parent to place a new teacher in such an awkward position. Most teachers assume you have cleared the decks with previous teachers and rarely will ask such a question at an interview/audition. Unpaid debts are an embarrassment to everyone involved.

SOME PERSONAL CONSIDERATIONS

A parent should note any personal habits that may interfere with a productive piano lesson. Besides attractive dress, both the teacher and studio should have a pleasant aroma. Children are sensitive to odors, such as body odors or bad breath, on the part of the teacher. Since a piano teacher sits near the student at the keyboard, your child will be aware if such a situation exists. Do not expect a successful relationship if the teacher offends the student with unpleasant personal habits. The reverse is also true: your child should be taught how to avoid offending the teacher.

Chewing gum is not acceptable at a piano lesson. It is a distraction to both teacher and student. Imagine trying to teach a student a solo in 4/4 rhythm, when he is chewing in waltz time!

Another thing, students should not wear long fingernails. They damage piano keys and case and are a handicap to finger technique. For the fingers to strike the keys properly, nails should be no longer than the end of the finger.

Rings and bracelets are not good companions when playing the piano. Jewelry will mar both your piano and the teacher's piano, besides inhibiting the use of fingers and arms. If worn to school, jewelry must be removed at the lesson. Hopefully it will be put back on again afterwards, or the teacher will have the annoying responsibility of keeping a "lost and found" department for forgetful children.

If you have questions or concerns about the progress of your child, call the teacher when he isn't teaching, or make an appointment to talk with him at his convenience. Do *not* discuss a problem when the child is listening! A teacher cannot be frank with you if the child is present. If the teacher should be open with you and the child were listening, such a discussion could cause discouragement in the child.

It is unwise and unnecessary to discuss what you consider to be shortcomings of former piano teachers with a new teacher. It is quite unethical for a teacher to participate in such a conversation. Belaboring any defects or oversights of the past, degenerates into malicious gossip and is of no benefit to anyone.

Keep one thing in mind at all times during a course of piano study. The teacher is a professional who is providing you with a professional service. Respect this and instill this respect in the child. It is superb training for him to conduct himself professionally also.

PART III: THE INSTRUMENT

CHAPTER 9

A CRASH COURSE IN PIANOS

"My grandmother had a hand-carved cherry wood piano; it sounded like bells. . ."

"Everybody KNOWS that an older piano has a better tone."

"Won't you please come over and tell us what you think of the piano we just bought?"

". . . and there where the shadows fall, I've planned to have a magnificent concert grand. . ."

— from *Vagabond's House* by Don Blanding

A BRIEF HISTORY OF THE INSTRUMENT

The piano is the most complete of all instruments. It requires no additional players or accompaniment to produce a performance. It can stand alone. The many other instruments used in orchestras and bands require either a piano accompaniment or a group situation.

Its correct name is the *pianoforte*, the Italian words for soft *(piano)* and loud *(forte)*. It is an instrument which can produce different intensities of sound, as well as differences in touch, such as legato (smooth, connected) and staccato (detached, quick).

Today's piano differs greatly from its predecessors — the virginal, clavichord and harpsichord. These earlier instruments produced a pitched tone, but were unable to substantially vary the intensity of sound. Virginals and clavichords produced very delicate sounds. The larger harpsichords produced a much greater sound, particularly if they had two strings, rather than one per note. In a clavichord, a small metal mallet *hits* the string. The action of a harpsichord *plucks* the string, producing an almost guitar-like quality of sound.

The pianoforte, which was invented around 1709 by Christofori, an Italian, uses an altogether different mechanical approach than either

45

the clavichord or harpsichord. The piano produces sound by having a felt hammer strike the string, or strings. Most pianos have three strings per note in the middle and treble sections of the scale. The very lowest notes have a single, large string, and the upper bass section has two strings. The average piano has about 250 strings. Depending on the force with which a key is depressed, the intensity of sound can change from soft to loud. Because of its unique construction, the sound of one tone can be sustained either by finger or pedal, until another tone replaces that tone. This allows a performer to achieve a legato melodic line, more like the human voice which can glide from one pitch to another.

Obviously, these radical changes in a keyboard instrument opened up an entirely new field to both composers and performers. Bach played on a pianoforte and liked it! The problem, at that early date, was keeping the then fragile instrument in tune. It required frequent adjustments during a concert. By supporting the tension of the strings with a sturdy metal frame capable of withstanding the enormous stress of about 17 to 20 tons, the present day piano emerged.

Much of Mozart's later piano music, particularly his Fantasies, obviously were written for the piano, although many of his compositions could be played on either a harpsichord or a piano. Beethoven's greatest sonata, the Opus 106 was sub-titled the *Hammerklavier*, the German word for pianoforte. He wanted to make it very clear that that particular sonata *had* to be played on a pianoforte.

The enormous wealth of composition for the piano is substantial testimony that the instrument gained rapidly in popularity with both composers and audiences. Less than 100 years after its creation, giants of the keyboard such as Clementi, Czerny, Busoni and Liszt began to explore the almost limitless possibilities of creating wonderful solos for the piano. There is more solo literature written for piano than for any other musical instrument.

The name pianoforte must have seemed too long, for now the majority of people refer to it as the *piano*. Some music reviewers have felt it should have been abbreviated to the *forte*, since so many amateur and professional pianists have a tendency to thrash it soundly in concert!

Whatever you call it, the pianoforte or piano is a sublime, complete instrument that affords familiarity with all pitches of tone, intensity of sound, and harmonic changes, as well as being the major instrument for solo performance.

NOT ALL PIANOS ARE THE SAME

The choices of pianos are many, and can be confusing to the non-pianist. There are over 50 brands of pianos on the market today. Prices range from a few hundred dollars to many thousands of dollars, depending on the size and quality.

Various factories make nothing but the special components of pianos, such as the action, the keyboard, keys, hammers, and felt to manufacturer's specifications. Others produce the cast metal plates necessary for pianos. Several name-brand pianos will purchase a certain quality action and plate from such factories made to their specifications, and use them in their own cabinet design, with whatever added features they desire for a specific price of piano. Only a few piano manufacturers make the entire instrument from frame to finished case.

SMALL PIANOS

The smallest of the vertical pianos is a *spinet*. This is an attractive piece of furniture, but should not be purchased for a serious piano student. Any piano less than 40" high will not produce a quality sound, the touch will be very light, and would be satisfactory only for those who use a piano rarely.

Some companies manufacture a mini-piano which has a shortened keyboard. Such instruments would be satisfactory only for someone who wanted a piano at Christmas-time for carol singing or for other limited-use occasions. Such an instrument will not sustain the heavy use of a good piano student, nor suffice for a performance of solo material.

STANDARD VERTICAL PIANOS

The most common vertical piano today is a model referred to as a *console*, or *vertical* (p. 49). This instrument is 40" to 42" high, will easily fit into today's smaller homes, and many times can be a very good value. It is certainly adequate for a piano student. The *studio* model (p. 50), usually around 44" to 46" high, is used in practice rooms and studios of universities and conservatories. It does not require any more home space than a console, but produces a much greater tone, and has greater key depth of touch. Some higher priced studio models possess a *sostenuto* pedal, which is a very desirable feature. The studio model is the best choice outside of buying a traditional 52"-high piano (or upright, p. 51), or best of all, a grand piano.

GRAND PIANOS

Grand pianos are of a totally different design. The strings are stretched horizontally instead of vertically, as in a vertical or console model. As a general rule, a grand piano should be at least 5' long to compare favorably with the professional or studio model.

Despite the common usage of such terms as "baby grand" or "parlor grand," these names refer to size, which depends on individual manufacturers. The names were attached to various sized grand pianos by enterprising salesmen or advertising departments, and they stuck. A "baby grand" (p. 52) could be anywhere from 4'6" to 5'6", a "parlor grand" anywhere from 6' to 7' in length. In between are medium grands (p. 53), often called "living room" or "music room" grands, which have ample string and soundboard length to provide a rich tone.

Each manufacturer produces varying sizes of grand pianos and signifies their size by letter or number. A large grand piano (p. 54) referred to as a "parlor grand" in times past, measures 6' to 7'. Many pianists choose a 7' to 7'6" piano for their home, because usually it has better balance of tone production between treble and bass. For many amateurs, as well as fine artists, this 7' grand can be the only instrument they ever own. It can be housed easily in a large living room and is a superb instrument.

The *concert grand* (p. 55), the ultimate, is 9' long, and is the size used on stages in concert by professional artists. The advantage of the long string length, and huge soundboard of a concert grand is obvious. It produces a much greater, as well as a more beautiful tone. There are many concert grands in private homes, but they require a very large room, both for the bulk and the acoustics of such a large instrument. The majority of concert grand pianos used by major symphonies and in concert halls are the Steinway, Boesendorfer and Baldwin. Many major orchestras have more than one concert grand available, as many artists perform only on a certain manufacturers instrument.

THE CONSOLE MODEL

A vertical piano between 40" and 42" high, the console comes in a wide range of styles and finishes, and is adequate for a piano student. The illustrated model is 40" high.

THE STUDIO MODEL

Usually between 44″ and 46½″ high, the studio piano is used in practice rooms of universities and conservatories, and is suitable for home or studio. The illustrated model is 46½″ high.

50

THE UPRIGHT MODEL
This traditional piano is 52" high, with a string length and soundboard size equal to a medium grand piano, giving it the fullest sound of all the verticals.

THE BABY GRAND

The smallest grand piano, between 4'6" and 5'6", fits well in a small living room. Most grands are available in a variety of furniture styles. The illustrated model is 5'1" long.

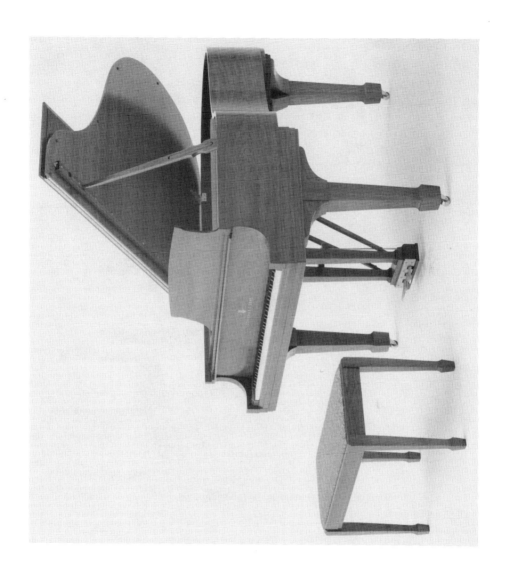

THE MEDIUM GRAND

Grand pianos measuring from 5'7" to 6', often called "living room" or "music room" grands, have ample string and soundboard length to provide a rich tone. The illustrated model is 5'7½" long.

THE LARGE GRAND

Pianos from 6' to 7'6", sometimes referred to as "parlor" grands, can be housed easily in a large living room, and are favored by many artists for their personal home piano. The illustrated model is 7' long.

54

THE CONCERT GRAND

Approximately 9' in length, these pianos produce a great and beautiful tone that fills a very large room or auditorium, and are used by major symphonies and in concert halls.

BENCHES AND CHAIRS

New pianos come equipped with a piano bench. This is ususally adequate for the beginning student (unless they are very young, such as age four). If legs and feet dangle, it is uncomfortable, but a footstool can ease this situation. The bench height may have to be altered to accommodate the tall child, thus an adjustable chair is a good solution (p. 52).

The most desirable seating is the artist bench (p. 55), which allows for height adjustment by knobs on either side of the padded bench to raise or lower the height. These are used in concert halls, and are available to anyone. They are expensive, but a wonderful answer to the varying heights of young people. A good piano studio should have an adjustable bench or chair, to have proper seating for different size children. *Never* use an arm chair at a piano!

THE PEDALS

There are three pedals on most pianos. They are the *una corda* on the left, the *sostenuto* in the middle (on grands and a few fine uprights), and the *damper* to the far right.

The *una corda* softens or lightens a tone. On upright pianos, the mechanism moves closer to the strings, thereby shortening the distance the hammer travels to hit the strings and produce a tone. This makes the sound less intense. On a grand piano, this pedal shifts the entire keyboard so that the hammers do not hit all of the strings that produce the tone.

The *sostenuto* pedal sustains or holds the sound of a note while both hands are playing additional notes in other areas of the keyboard. Many uprights do not possess this pedal, and several European pianos, verticals or grands, do not have it at all. Impressionistic composers such as Debussy and Ravel, as well as jazz pianists, use this pedal as a very effective device. The sostenuto pedal is not as essential as the other two pedals and a young student would have little use for it in the beginning.

The function of the *damper* (sustaining) pedal is to lift or remove the felt dampers from *all* the strings so that a key, when struck, may have the full benefit of the sympathetic vibrations of the entire soundboard. It will allow a tone to continue sounding, even though the finger has been removed from the keyboard. Commonly called the "loud" pedal, it is dreadfully over-used, creating a mushy, hazy sound in an otherwise lovely composition.

The pedals are connected to the piano mechanism by metal rods. These also have felt bushings to avoid squeaks or thumps resulting from friction wearing out the felt fittings. Adjusting or repairing pedal function must be done by a piano technician.

The usage of pedals is inadequately taught in many cases. Paderewski called the damper pedal the "soul of the piano." Perhaps this is true, but the use of the damper pedal will *not* cover mistakes nor wrong notes; it will merely muddy the sound if not used properly. Depressing it, and knowing when to release it, so as to recapture new harmony with a fresh pedal, is part of the artistry of a fine pianist.

CHAPTER 10

GETTING THE PIANO

SHOULD YOU BUY OR RENT?

If there is great doubt in your mind that your child is at all interested in piano lessons, or if a geographical move is imminent, renting is a good solution. Otherwise, buy a piano.

Should you decide that renting is best for your circumstances, do rent from a reputable piano dealer. Most dealers have arrangements for rentals, and many of them will apply your rent toward the purchase of the rental piano or a larger piano. Usually the renter will be required to pay the cartage of the piano to and from his residence. Many piano dealers tune the piano before it is delivered into your home, and normally the tuning will not be affected by the move.

Either buying or renting, you are safest working with a reputable piano dealer. Merchants who wish to retain the goodwill of their customers, will stand behind their pianos.

BUYING THE BEST YOU CAN AFFORD

If you make a wise choice, it will probably be a permanent investment. Fine pianos hold their value, and many will actually increase in value. More importantly, you will be providing the necessary equipment for your child's piano lessons, as well as adding to the charm of your home.

Buying a piano demands some shopping around and consideration of what you want and can afford. Many young parents are not in a financial position to buy the piano of their dreams, and will purchase a good, but lesser piano, with the intent of changing it in the future. If money is no consideration, it is always better to buy the best and biggest piano you can for your home.

BUYING A USED INSTRUMENT

Buying a piano from a private party? Beware! If you see what appears to be a good buy advertised, first go see the instrument. Ask if you may have a piano technician check it over. If the owner objects, don't buy it. Paying a technician to inspect a piano is well worth the fee; he may save you hundreds of dollars and a great deal of grief. Keep in mind that you have no recourse when you buy from a private party. It can be even more embarrassing if you buy from a friend.

When you have the technician check the piano, your main concern is that the felts, bushings, hammers, strings, keys, bridges and soundboard are in good condition. Cracks in a soundboard are not necessarily detrimental. A qualified technician must make that judgment. Stress damage to bridges and pin blocks are not uncommon. However, there is an additional reason for having it checked before bringing it into your home. Unused or rarely played pianos are an attractive home for mice, moths and silverfish. These not only damage the instrument, but are quite unwelcome in your home.

Pianos which are rarely played should have moth crystals placed inside them. In a grand piano, place them inside at the back to lesson moth damage and discourage mice from nesting. In an upright piano, hang a bag of moth crystals inside the back of the piano. There have been many buyers from private parties who discovered afterwards that they brought infestation into their homes.

After buying the piano from a private party, you may find it needs a sizeable investment to make it usable. Only a technician can tell you ahead of time if everything is in good condition and working properly. Another pianist, or a piano teacher, can only assess the tone and the touch, but not the mechanics of a piano.

DON'T BUY FIRST AND ASK FOR AN OPINION AFTER

Several times in my teaching career, I received a phone call from a happy student or parent asking, "Won't you please come over and tell us what you think of the piano we just bought!? Hopefully, it *is* a good piano. But, that is not always the case.

Early in every teacher-pupil-parent relationship, I would stress that if they were considering the purchase of a piano, to let me know and/or have it checked by a technician. If they were buying from a reputable piano dealer, I had no concern. The private party sale is something else. All too frequently, a parent or student can look at a piano that has a fine finish, and looks splendid, only to find out it needs many internal parts repaired. Please do not find yourself in that situation. *Always* have a piano checked by a technician. Once you have it in your home, it is too late to consider the additional expense it may cause you.

RESTORED PIANOS

There are piano technicians and craftsmen who are capable of totally restoring and refinishing a piano. While they are rare, and may be difficult to find, these artisans exist. Their reputations will be well-known and respected in their area or community. Generally, they will use their considerable skills on grand pianos. A top-brand older piano that a family wishes to retain may be saved by excellent restoration. The purchase of a well-restored piano can result in a substantial saving over the price of a new piano. No ethical technician will waste his time, or your money, restoring a piano of questionable value.

COMMON PITFALLS

Grandmother's old upright poses a difficult problem. The case may be lovely, and the instrument may have great sentimental value. However, before you consider using such a piano, hire a piano technician to inspect it thoroughly. Find out what is necessary to replace or repair to make it a usable piano. The cost of replacing keys, felts, bushings, hammers or faulty strings may require more money than the old upright is worth.

Only once in my life have I seen an old upright that deserved total renovation. American friends in West Berlin had purchased an old upright piano shortly after WWII from a German piano teacher. It sounded dreadful. The strings were banging against each other, the pedals did not work and it was unusable. However, the case was so exquisite it was of museum qualtiy with a hand-carved cherrywood case and a hand-rubbed finish.

At my suggestion, they had it gutted, and replaced everything inside. When completed, it was a jewel of a piano, and has become a family treasure. This is the exception. Most older uprights are not of that case quality, and do not warrant any substantial investment in restoration.

CHAPTER 11
BRINGING HOME THE PIANO

MOVING ISN'T EASY!

Do *not* attempt to move a piano yourself. Besides being huge and heavy, pianos are complicated musical instruments and need to be handled by people who are trained to do it without harm. Most of the older uprights were made with an extremely heavy, cast metal plate to withstand the enormous stress created by stretching strings on it. It takes skilled manpower to manuever such a large weight delicately. For example, a 9' concert grand requires four trained movers to handle it safely.

If a piano is dropped or jostled too much, great damage can ensue. I have heard of pianos tipping off pickup trucks and other such horror stories. In such a case, nothing has been saved, and worse, additional repair expenses were created. It is well worth the money to hire qualified piano movers who carry insurance against damages.

PLACEMENT OF THE PIANO

Getting the piano established in your home is only the beginning. If you want your child to study piano successfully, the piano has to be placed in a location that will be conducive to uninterrupted daily practice.

Do not put the piano in a room where the child cannot use it without annoying other family members. The room where the TV is located is a bad location. Parents come home from work, and want to watch the news. The child has been in school all day, possibly with sports after school, and this seems to him the most logical time to practice.

The basement is not a good place for the piano. Learning a musical instrument is a lonely business anyway, and the child should not feel banished because he needs to practice. The basement can be harmful to the instrument as well as making practice time seem like punishment. Unfortunately, I have known parents who placed the piano in an *unheated* basement, where the student had to practice with gloves on! Now the child was not only alone, but cold.

Many of today's homes have been designed to be wonderful "entertaining houses." Everything is open and flowing from one room to another. This is wonderful, if all you do is give parties. However, it is a dreadful floor plan for the privacy of any family member, and absolute death for piano practicing. With these open plans, *everyone* must listen to piano practicing, and the student knows he has an audience. As a result, he will accomplish very little for fear of making a mistake that everyone hears.

If you truly want your child to enjoy, and learn to play the piano, there may have to be some adjustments to your lifestyle. A daily practice routine should be established. There should be a definite time every day, with rare exceptions for special events, when the student knows he can practice. A student should never be asked to "Shush" or practice softly.

Some parents can cope with the situation by having a small television in another room, so that while the child is practicing, they can relax. A child is very sensitive to making errors, and needs the opportunity to practice piano privately. Even if you have the finest teacher in the world, but make the availability of the piano difficult, very little will be accomplished.

Another serious consideration: a piano can't be situated just anywhere in a room. Temperature, humidity, and weather all affect the piano and its case. Vertical pianos should ideally be placed against an interior wall if possible, to minimize fluctuations in temperature. Allowing the sun to beat down on a piano will cause the finish to check and crack. Also, it will dry out the piano's felts and bushings much faster than should occur. *Never* place a grand piano over a heat outlet in the floor, or an upright instrument in front of a wall heat outlet. People and plants generate moisture which can be damaging to keys and strings. If a piano is placed in a bedroom, or in a room with several green plants, a small tubular heating unit should be used to dry the air.

Pianos require a certain humidity. In some areas, winters become very cold and dry. If homes are not equipped with a furnace which has an automatic humidifier as part of the heating system, free-standing humidifiers are recommended somewhere in the room, to provide proper humidity. In hotter areas, where there is both heat and high humidity, a de-humidifier is necessary. Check with your piano technician or piano dealer for advice on this. Do not wait for damage to occur.

After a piano has been moved and positioned in your home, it requires at least two weeks to adjust to the temperature and humidity of the new environment. After this, have a piano technician make any adjustments to the tuning if necessary. For further information, see the chapter on maintenance.

PIANOS ARE NOT TABLES NOR ART GALLERIES

The only thing that is acceptable on a piano, is music. Shawls, family pictures, vases of flowers and other bric-a-brac do not belong on a piano. Without meaning harm, I am sure, decorators suggest, and do such things. A piano is an expensive musical instrument, and should be treated as such. Many keyboards have been marred, chipped, or damaged by falling objects: damage can occur from a vase of flowers being tipped over.

Parties in the home present problems, since if any drinking is done around the piano, a slosh of liquid could find its way inside and do enormous damage. Water and piano interiors do not mix. Unless the party is to be a musical affair, the safest treatment of your piano is to close the lid and cover the keyboard. In the unhappy event that a water ring from a drinking glass, a cigarette burn, a damaged ivory, or liquid inside the piano ever occurs, *immediately* call your piano technician. He will know what to do to either erase, or minimize the damage. Sometimes it is necessary to have the lid totally refinished, strings replaced, or have the technician dry out the interior. This is all very costly and could be easily prevented with a little forethought.

CREATIVE WAYS TO RUIN A PIANO

Young children find it fascinating to "drive" little plastic or metal toys up and down a keyboard. You must protect the piano against these onslaughts, since serious damage can be done to the ivory or plastic keyboard. Little people (and grown-ups as well) should be restrained from pounding the keys with their fists, either to see what happens, or in frustration over practicing.

Many pianists suffer from perspiring hands and fingers. This gives the performer the sensation of skating on a slick film of water, and can be disconcerting. The best solution to this problem is for the pianist to carry a fine lawn or linen handkerchief, wiping the hands and keyboard between compositions. However, there *are* a few performers who actually spray a hair-setting lotion on the keys! This is a dreadful thing to do to a keyboard, and requires slow and careful cleaning to remove. The theory is that it will make the keyboard easier to hold onto, but can do damage not only to the surface of the key, but to the felt key-bed under the keys. This is *not* a recommended procedure!

If any decorating work is to be done in your home, the piano should be covered first with a soft blanket, and then a large piece of plastic. Many grand pianos have their own fitted flannel/felt covers. This is ideal. Plaster droppings from ceiling work, or paint specks require expensive cleaning and refinishing.

There are infinite ways to destroy the beauty of your instrument, both active and through neglect. Make a commitment to your investment. Protect it and be proud of it. Treat it with care and consideration and it will appreciate in value like a fine investment.

CHAPTER 12
A PIANO DOESN'T JUST SIT THERE

MAINTAINING YOUR PIANO

The possession or acquisition of a piano is only part of being a piano owner or renter. Pianos require maintenance. There are thousands of moving parts in a piano, and these will wear out and need replacement due to age or use. Everyone accepts the fact that an automobile will not stay trouble-free without regular care, such as tune-ups or replacement of batteries and new tires. A piano is just as complex and needs equal attention. Automobiles and pianos are two possessions that must be maintained whether or not they are used.

Cleaning is only part of good maintenance. The piano must be kept in tune. Pedals need adjustment, felts may need changing, the keys may need weighting, and from time to time, the piano will need voicing. Voicing is the shaping of the hammer to produce a clear, lovely sound. Deeply grooved hammers require attention, as a good clean surface is not striking the strings properly.

FINDING A GOOD TECHNICIAN

There are three ways to find a qualified piano technician in your area. If you live in a metropolitan area, call the local symphony office and find out who cares for the piano used by the orchestra and visiting pianists. Check with the major piano dealer in your area for the name or names of qualified technicians. Third and perhaps most important, a personal recommendation from a pianist you admire and respect is desirable. A non-pianist's opinion is of little value, but a pianist can tell you how a piano responds and holds up after being worked on by a technician.

KEEPING THE INSTRUMENT TUNED

When a piano is tuned, the tension of each string is adjusted to a correct pitch. Today, pianos are tuned to a 440 A, which means that the A above middle C must vibrate at 440 vibrations per second.

The pitch of a piano is essential to the quality of the sound, as well as proper ear training of the pianist. The piano you play will become the standard by which you judge all other pianos.

All pianos must be tuned on a regular basis. In most parts of the world, a tuning will last six months, and usually longer, if a piano is not moved. In a climate where there are great fluctuations of temperature and humidity, a piano will require more frequent tunings. If a piano is left untuned for several years, there is a great risk of having strings break when pulled up to pitch. Replacing strings is a special technique.

It is unfortunate, but many people believe tuning is a simple thing that can be done by nearly anybody with the right tools. True, many people can be taught to adjust string tension, but it requires a trained piano technician to produce a lovely tone and adjust the string tension so that one note corresponds correctly to the next. This ensures that intervals (the distance between two tones), are uniform.

There is a great controversy about tuning by ear and tuning with an electronic device. There are piano technicians who can produce magnificent results with either method; unfortunately there are those who achieve entirely unsatisfactory results also. It is imperative to research the reputation of anyone you hire to tune your piano.

VOICING (REGULATING) A PIANO

This procedure is the delicate task of shaping and adjusting the hammers so they will strike the strings at the proper density to produce a fine sound. It must be done by a qualified technician. Only he can produce an equal scale so that one note corresponds in volume and tone quality to the next.

Many "tuners" are not qualified for this work. All piano hammers are made of pure wool felt which must be softened or hardened to produce evenness of tone. Over a period of time and use, the hammers on any piano will become harder and harder through the repeated striking of the strings. The powerful force exerted by the mechanism causes the felt hammers to develop grooves from striking the strings repeatedly. The technician will need to reshape the hammer with a special file to obtain a clean striking surface. Also, he may need to prick the felt hammers with a special tool to adjust and soften the tone quality, so it is not harsh, but clear and beautiful.

If left untended, hammers can become so hard as to sound metallic and very unpleasant to the ear. A valid indication that a piano requires voicing can be noted by the layman by a harsh, tinny sound. This greatly diminishes the pleasure of either playing or listening to a piano. Eventually, a piano that has had great use will need to have the entire set of hammers replaced. Again, this requires great skill on the part of the piano technician.

PEDAL ADJUSTMENT AND REPAIR

Periodically, a pedal or pedals will need attention from a technician. The most common problem is the development of a squeak or thump, which usually is due to the wearing of the felt bushings where the metal rods attach to the piano mechanism. Occasionally, a damper pedal will not release as soon as pressure on it is removed. This creates the continuation of sounds the pianist does not intend. Frequently, young children have damaged the function of pedals, by depressing them with heavy toys, or other games. While this should not be allowed, only a technician can rectify the situation.

KEY WEIGHT

A fairly firm touch on a piano is desirable. It allows a pianist to use his individual abilities to create gradations of tone volume and quality of sound. Occasionally, one will find an instrument where the touch is so heavy to depress that it seems impossible to play comfortably, particularly for young children. If that is the case, a trained technician can adjust the touch.

There are small lead weights inside the wooden body of a key which can be added or removed so as to alter the touch. Some older pianos have a light action and require scarcely more than a feather touch. This is not desirable for a student as it will not develop a strong pianist, and will often make him feel he can play *only* on his own piano. Obviously, this is impractical. Pianists, of all musicians, must develop a technique that will allow them to perform on *any* piano. Unlike other orchestral and band instruments, a pianist cannot take his piano with him whenever he performs.

An exception would be a great artist such as Vladimir Horowitz, who always traveled with his own 9' concert grand Steinway, and his own personal technician. Horowitz practiced on a fairly heavy-action piano, but preferred performing on a lighter-touch piano. He felt this allowed for greater speed and delicacy.

When one is a very great artist, many things are possible. Josef Hoffman had a very small hand. Because of this physical problem, he had special pianos made for him by Steinway, where they shaved the width of each key slightly. This made it possible for Hoffman to perform compositions by Chopin and Liszt which required large stretches of the hand.

It is not uncommon in coastal or humid areas, for a piano action to feel very heavy. Sometimes this is due to friction in the moving parts, rather than key weights. Usually it is not necessary to alter the weight of a key.

CLEANING

Pianos require daily dusting, and as with all finely finished furniture, dusting should be done in the direction of the wood grain. In addition, the piano needs regular cleaning of both the keys and the cabinet. If you have bought a new piano, the dealer will instruct you how to care for the finish of the case of the instrument. The Steinway piano with a satin finish, for example, is wiped clean with a cloth wrung out very dry in clear water, then buffed with a soft, dry cloth. Similar cleaning is used on the gloss finish of pianos, such as a polyester/polymer finish.

Too many pianos are sprayed with polishes that actually attract dirt, rather than enhance the finish. For most piano cases, either the water cleaning method, or a very light polish with lemon oil will give the best results.

Keys need frequent washing. Soil and perspiration from hands will accumulate on the key surface and needs to be removed. This is best done by using a damp cloth and mild soap, and stroking each key carefully, then drying them individually.

Frequently, pianists are asked to perform in a lovely home, perhaps on a fine instrument. If the owners are not musicians, it does not occur to them how unpleasant it is for a pianist to play on a dirty keyboard. Many pianists carry a damp cloth with them for such situations.

Pianos accumulate dust, inside as well as outside. Besides a daily dusting, the interior needs to be vacuumed on a regular basis. This should be done with great care. When dusting the dampers with a vacuum brush attachment, you should be very careful not to disturb the position of the damper on the three strings. *Never* brush crosswise on the dampers, but use a light stroke in the direction of the string length.

With spinets and many uprights or smaller pianos, interior cleaning is best done by your technician, since certain styles of construction make it difficult for the owner to clean without incurring damage.

REFINISHING OR PAINTING A PIANO

To paint a piano is unthinkable to me, but there are people who decide their instrument would look better if it matched their decor, rather than being black or a wood finish.

Colored pianos are not unknown. On a visit to the Steinway factory in Hamburg, Germany, I saw five concert grand pianos being readied for shipment to China. They were finished in a brilliant, glossy red! Nearby, was an instrument finished in a delicate mauve shade. They were quite startling.

Musical instruments are not just pieces of furniture. A piano, violin, guitar, or other instrument, does not need to color coordinate with the furnishings. Matching woods is not difficult since many choices of wood are available for pianos. The most common for the large grand pianos is black, with either a satin or glossy finish. The majority of large pianos made in Russia, the Orient, and many European countries are now finished in a highly polished black polyester/polymer finish. For the smaller grand pianos, and many styles of uprights, mahogany, walnut or rosewood are the most common choices.

If you have an old piano with a marred finish, refinishing it will greatly enhance its appearance. If you decide to paint, if you must do it, don't try to do it yourself. If things go wrong, as they often do, you will have a situation which requires even greater expense to rectify. Hire a professional refinisher.

Whatever the finish of your instrument, treat it well. A fine piano will hold its value for a lifetime with proper maintenance and care.

PART IV: THE LESSONS

CHAPTER 13
TYPES OF LESSONS

THE PRIVATE LESSON

The private piano lesson is the ideal way for a young person to learn. Your child may be treated individuallly, with consideration given to his special gifts or problems, age, size of hands, and physical, mental and musical abilities. Each child can progress at his own speed, according to his capabilities. Lesson material may be selected especially for him, and his needs, as he develops piano skills.

The complete attention a teacher can give to one child is most desirable. A part of our educational problems have arisen due to the large number of children in school classrooms. There is little doubt that the individual child can benefit from a private teacher. In classrooms, this is completely impossible, and schools endeavor to group students by ability in various ways. However, with piano, you *can* have a private teacher, and it is the most effective way to learn.

A parent is paying for a private lesson, and should expect very personal attention paid to his child at such a lesson. It is the last example of the private tutorial method of teaching in our present society. Because of the intimate nature of a private piano lesson, a child can make dramatic progress if he has the capability of learning. I believe the private lesson is a valuable tool in child development. At least, in one area of his learning process, he is treated as an individual, and not part of a class. The greater the ability of the child, the more crucial it is to provide private piano lessons at the earliest opportunity.

CLASS LESSONS — AN OPTIONAL BEGINNING

Class piano lessons can be a very pleasant way to start piano. If the teacher meets all the requirements of credentials, personality and studio, it can be a viable option. Many students can benefit from being in a class with a small number of students, to learn some of the basic knowledge of the keyboard and printed page of music.

An ideal time for such a beginning is summer vacation. The child will be free of school obligations, and attending a class piano lesson with others his age can be a delightful introduction to the piano.

Class lessons start losing their value after about three months. At that time, each pupil is beginning to exhibit his individual abilities. Some children are able to go at a much faster rate than others. As with any class, the work is commonly geared to the slowest student. Consequently, class piano lessons are fine, for a *limited* period of time. After six weeks to three months, confer with the teacher and find out how the child is progressing. If he obviously is able to progress more rapidly than the class, then start your search for a good private teacher. The class teacher may also maintain a private studio. If not, he should be able to supply some names of qualified teachers who teach private piano lessons.

The initial value of class piano lessons is that the child does not feel so alone, and that he is with others of his own age, learning new information. It can be a pleasant game situation. If class piano lessons are used in this limited way, the child may be more receptive to an individual lesson where he may progress at his own rate of speed. Advancement will come only with a good private teacher, who is teaching your child as an individual.

ROTE PIANO LESSONS

Rote piano lessons are another type of piano study. I believe they present some problems that should be considered. There are several methods being used today to teach a child to play piano by hearing music repeatedly, and then "finding" it on the keyboard. Parents who want to give their child the advantages of piano lessons will be intrigued by the availability of such lessons that will start children as early as age three!

Personally, I cannot recommend this type of teaching for a number of reasons. Mainly, the very young child, unless he is a rare genius, does not have the working knowledge of letters and numbers necessary to learn to read music. His motor muscles are still quite undeveloped, and his attention span is short. He is a baby.

It is quite possible to attend recitals of students, who have been taught by a rote method, and be overwhelmed by the fluency of some of the students. One can listen to a program like this, and be convinced that rote teaching must be successful. Children *can* learn quite a bit of music by rote, and master several short pieces easily. After all, children are master mimics. As long as the composition adheres to a simple form, such as Part A, Part B, and a repeat of Part A, the musically inclined piano student can learn and remember the piece, without reading notes. I have heard rote students perform short pieces, and Clementi and Kuhlau sonatinas (usually first movements only) and been impressed.

So what's the problem? The piano student reaches a plateau of learning. He now has the facility with his fingers to study the standard keyboard repertoire, but he can't *read* music or reads very poorly. This will be denied by those teachers who teach rote lessons, and I believe they are sincere in believing that they do incorporate reading music in the lessons. Some of the pupils taught in this fashion will comprehend and make the connection between that black spot on a piece of paper and a location on the keyboard. There are others who will never understand that association or be able to make the transition to reading, and that *is* a big problem.

In reality, this method reverts to the old days of the use of "Dick and Jane" readers in the early grades of school These books taught children to recognize the *shape* of a word. Such words as "many, money, mealy, mushy" all start with an "m" and have a "tail" at the end. While some children learned to read by the "Dick and Jane" method, this period in our schools produced thousands of children who either didn't learn, or emerged as poor readers. Until the child started having problems with reading, he was not given the principles of language construction. Usually only a child in remedial reading was taught the complex usage of vowels and consonants.

I have had several rote-taught piano students come to me when they were about 12 years old. They were capable of playing a limited amount of piano music, but had the finger dexterity to advance to more difficult music. Seldom was I successful with helping a student make the transition from listening-learning to reading-learning. To learn to *read* music, a student would have to regress to simpler pieces. This made him feel stupid and incompetent. As a result, he would pursue piano lessons for a brief time, and then "become too busy to study" any more.

For reasons I do not understand, the rote method *appears* to be more successful with violin students. Perhaps imitating or "finding" a tone on a string is far different than finding a definite place on a keyboard. This is hard for me to accept, as I studied violin for six years as a child and found it much simpler to locate a note on the keyboard, than to slide up and down on a string to match a certain pitch of tone. Initially, rote lessons were used with stringed instruments only. Violin music uses only one clef, not two clefs as piano music does. Violin is either reading, or finding, a single note at a time in elementary violin. Piano music uses two clefs, both hands, and very early in lessons, a pupil will be playing several notes with each hand and both hands together. Neither the instrument, nor its music, offer a reasonable comparison of problems.

The origin of the most popular rote method is Asian. In general, the Asiatic approach to all learning, and life endeavors is more committed than that of the European-American approach to learning. The compelling need to excel is associated with family honor, and pride in accomplishment. Even with such an ethnic background, and commitment to succeed, a plateau will be reached, where learning to *read* music fluently must be mastered. I wish I could see this urgent sense of achievement in *all* students and parents.

The lesson approach to rote learning is quite different than that of reading-learning. The parents are encouraged to attend rote lessons with the child and to take personal responsibility that sufficient practicing is done. There is a definite sense of duty that is more compelling with Asian people than it is with European-American people. It is possible the latter do not ask, nor expect, as much from their children, as they should.

My conclusion is that rote learning will work for a limited time. However, it puts a stone wall in front of the child. When the inevitable time comes where the pupil must learn to read music to go further, the printed page has become a monster to him. It is impractical, if not altogether impossible, to learn a 40-page Beethoven sonata just by listening to it over and over. Occasionally, one will read of an outstanding rote-taught student performing a concert, or winning a competition. It is in the newspaper because it *is* news — not the norm.

I cannot see the advantage of teaching a child to play piano by one method, and then telling him he must learn another method to proceed further. The printed page of piano music is a complicated set of symbols, notes, rests, phrase marks, and directions by the composer. The only way to comprehend printed music is to learn from the beginning how to read it correctly and accurately. When many rote students reach the impasse of needing to change methods, they too may join the ranks of those who say "I used to take piano lessons when I was younger, but of course, I can't play a thing now."

CHAPTER 14

WHAT TO EXPECT FROM LESSONS

INGREDIENTS OF A GOOD LESSON

Both parent and student deserve to know what to expect from a private piano lesson. Both of you anticipate many things, and a parent has the right to attend an occasional lesson to observe what takes place. Here are some things that make up a good lesson:

The lesson will be an organized, private tutoring session between the student and the professional teacher. The lesson will begin with whatever technical exercises have been assigned—finger drills, scales, arpeggios, and the many difficult physical problems that need to be mastered. The majority of good piano lessons will cover technique, sonata material, and solo material. Usually small sections of each will be heard, corrected, and improved.

The student will first be allowed to play through a section of what has been assigned at the previous lesson. Major corrections of notes and rhythmic patterns must be made by the teacher. No student should be sent away without knowing what basic things he is doing wrong. But, if a student is stopped for a long discourse after playing just a few measures, the teacher is not permitting the student to show what he has accomplished.

Only so much material can be covered in a lesson and no good teacher will attempt to cover an entire sonata, as well as other technical and solo material in a 45-minute lesson. That would be a waste of the student's time, as it allows for no corrections or comments. An exception is the rare lesson time when a student is performing an entire program and the teacher needs to hear it from beginning to end.

Many piano teachers will illustrate a certain passage by playing it for the student. This is most common with the student who has little or no experience with the style of a certain composer. Such teacher illustrations should be used sparingly. If too frequent, the student will attempt to copy, rather than learn how to achieve that effect himself.

78

The younger the student, the more imperative it is for a teacher to encourage and praise, if at all possible. Lessons cannot be taught without criticism, but criticism can be of a positive nature.

No student should be sent away from a lesson without a positive feeling of capability. Even if praise must be meager, it must be present. Students need encouragement from a teacher. Only when a student has been rebellious and has not practiced, should a teacher scold a student. Under those circumstances, the student expects it, as he knows he is at fault.

At no time should there be any physical coercion by the teacher. Pencils should never be rapped across a student's knuckles, nor should a teacher ever resort to shaking a child. Any teacher who resorts to such behavior should be replaced immediately..

A good piano lesson will be a time of information and encouragement to achieve higher levels of performance. It is a weekly inspiration session, which should whet the appetite of the student to try harder.

WHAT SHOULD BE LEARNED THE FIRST YEAR

If you have chosen a teacher wisely and the child is of an age to learn and benefit from piano lessons, the following should have been learned in the first year of lessons:

1. Awareness of keyboard—how many octaves?

2. Arrangements of notes on keyboard—groups of black notes in twos and threes.

3. Treble clef and bass clef signs.

4. Names of the lines and spaces of both treble and bass clefs, and where those notes are on the keyboard.

5. Association of keyboard note location with how it looks on the printed page of music.

6. Rhythmic value of notes—whole, half, quarter, eighth and sixteenth

7. Bar lines (measure lines).

8. Recognition and value of rest signs.

9. Phrase marks and what they mean.

10. Recognition of sharp (#) and flat (b) signs, and how to sharp or flat a note on the keyboard.

11. Legato and staccato touch on the keyboard, and the marks that indicate each touch.

12. Ear training—recognizing high and low sounds, and recognition of intervals of an octave, a 3rd, 4th and 5th.

13. Time signature—recognizing the top number gives the number of beats in a measure, and the lower signifies the type of note receiving one full count.

14. Structure of a simple solo form, e.g., ABA, AB and Coda, ABCA, etc.

15. Memory training—knowledge of a solo's form which aids memorization.

16. Recognizing repeat signs.

17. Ability to perform a simple piece within a 2-octave range on the keyboard.

18. Knowing the full name and composer of a solo.

19. Always knowing the last chord or note of a piece.

20. Knowing the names and function of the pedals—*una corda, sostenuto,* and *damper.*

21. Knowing the full name and explanation of the instrument's name — *pianoforte* (soft-loud).

That is a formidable list of information and underlines the necessity of the student having letter and number skills. However, after a full year of instruction, the student should know this information.

CHAPTER 15

THE LESSON MATERIALS

"We just want June to play for Sunday School, so does she really need all this other stuff?"

"I know she isn't going to major in music in college, so can you just skip the scales and Bach?"

A BRIEF BACKGROUND

When this country was young, Americans desperately wanted music and culture in their lives. Fine instruction in the arts at that time was restricted to the very few who had the money, talent and good fortune to live on the East Coast. Some were able to travel to Europe for instruction, but thousands were not able to do so.

The European approach consisted of studying technique, technique and more technique. When mastery of the keyboard was achieved, then a student was allowed to start learning the vast repertoire of piano literature that was desired and accepted in the concert halls of Europe and the U.S.A.

As our nation expanded westward, a phenomenon occurred which would affect the teaching of piano from that time to the present day. Our hardy pioneers were dragging their square grand pianos across the mountains and plains in covered wagons, or shipping them around the Horn of South America to the West Coast. Those Americans who settled in the mid-section of our country wanted music for themselves and their children. They didn't want to study years and years of technique before being able to play music. Most of them were not considering a concert career. They just wanted someone to play that piano that they had wrestled into Mid-America.

There was then a whole new world of *customers* erupting with this increase of people who wanted to play the piano. But there was also a vast void of piano teaching materials. Into this situation came a group of sincere musicians, who recognized a "pot of gold" if they could put together materials that could be used by the less-proficient teacher and pianist. The concept of Methods Courses had arrived.

Piano teachers were the authors of the early piano Methods Books. They introduced a new concept of piano teaching. Now, education and culture were being made available to *all*, not just a few talented or wealthy citizens. Obviously, piano educational material was kept at a reasonable level of accomplishment. "Better to light one candle than curse the darkness," and most certainly, the piano candle had been lit!

METHODS BOOKS

There are numerous methods books available for piano teachers to use. Some of the early methods books, such as *John Thompson* and the *Progressive Piano Series*, are still in use. In recent years, a plethora of methods have appeared. A few examples are books by Pace, Glover, and Leila Fletcher, but the list is almost endless. They are extremely popular, as they can be used by almost anyone with modest ability on the piano.

What many people do not know is that methods books are written for the mass market. Since they must adapt to the ability level of the majority, they move slowly. As in class lessons, the material is adapted to the slowest student in the class, leaving the highly talented and intelligent piano student feeling stifled.

Method books are not bad, but they should be used *in addition to* other materials. If your child is on the third or fourth John Thompson book with no additional materials, he and you are being cheated out of the great keyboard literature he should be learning. This often happens with piano teachers who are unfamiliar with the fine piano solos written by great composers for children, and some piano teachers who teach class lessons.

The majority of piano teachers *do* begin with a method book, but will rapidly augment this with additional material, covering technique, sonatina and sonata literature, and solo material. These beginning books provide a relatively easy way to introduce a young student to the five-foot-wide keyboard, and what a note looks like on paper, in relationship to where it is on the piano. But, if your child is studying piano from a methods book, and that is *all* he has, do start looking for another teacher.

TEACHING PIECES AND SIMPLIFIED MUSIC

Because many piano teachers are not familiar with the huge repertoire of great piano literature for children, a large amount of piano "teaching pieces" have reached the market. Piano students who are quite capable of learning a Bach minuet, a Clementi sonatina, or one of the small pieces by Grieg, Schumann, Haydn, or Beethoven, are being fed a horrible diet of dreadful solos. A few examples of current solos on the market are "Landing of the Moon Men," "Dance of the Freaks," "The Elephant's Waltz," and "The March of the Chocolate Chip Cookies."

Many years ago, some piano teachers decided to make "simplified editions" of advanced piano literature. This practice has been carried to the extreme. Beginning students will play the "Tschaikowsky Piano Concerto," which consists of the main theme in a very simplified rendition. Both student and parent are being deceived with simplified piano solos. They should *never* be used. There is more appropriate material available than they can ever master and great piano music should not be demeaned in such a fashion.

All piano students should work on *original* editions of whatever they are playing. Simplified editions of great piano music are insulting to both composer and student. Reducing great music to the banal, is akin to rewriting Dickens, Poe, or Mark Twain.

APPROPRIATE SOLO AND STUDY LITERATURE

Even the beginning student should be exposed to the small, charming compositions of many great composers, such as Bach, Beethoven, Mozart, Haydn, Grieg and Schumann. All these composers, and many others, wrote pieces specifically for the young pianist.

The young student is quite capable of learning fine music right from the beginning of his piano study. Part of the reason such fine solo material is avoided by some teachers, is the familiarity of the pieces. Well-known, often-heard compositions are recognizable even by non-pianists. Audiences can hear when a mistake has been made.

Teaching the standard keyboard repertoire puts the teacher in the situation where he *must* teach it correctly. Any teacher using such material is subjecting himself to possible criticism, if incorrect notes or rhythm occur in a student's performance. All too frequently, teachers remove themselves from that position of being criticized, by teaching relatively unknown compositions. Much of the time, the audience has never heard it before and will not know how it is supposed to sound.

If you ever attend a lesson or recital and do not recognize a single title or composer on the program, you should question the teacher's qualifications. The quality piano teacher will rely heavily on the great store-house of music written by well-known composers.

There is more great piano literature available than most pianists can cover in a lifetime. To begin enjoying and playing this wonderful music, students must be led through less difficult music first. Most pianists will endeavor to read all the great piano music written, but it would be impossible to achieve a polished performance on the entire amount.

At the present time, there are excellent teaching materials available. There are many collections of original solos by various great composers compiled by *The Alfred Masterwork Series*, Frances Clark, Palmer editions of sonatinas and sonatas, Palmer editions of individual composers, Fischer Collections and Anson Collections of Sonatinas and Sonatas are just a few of the splendid teaching tools without which all teachers would suffer.

BOYS AND GIRLS LIKE DIFFERENT MUSIC

Piano teachers must take into consideration the difference of material suitable for a boy, and what is suitable for a girl. Girls will willingly play solos named "Swaying Daffodils" or "The Fairy's Dance," but such solos will make any normal nine-year-old boy squirm. He just won't get up in front of his peers and play such pieces. It makes him feel foolish, and like a sissy. Teachers must take into account the sex and temperament of a student before assigning solo material. As there is a wealth of fine piano music young people can learn and play, there is no reason to use solos with silly names.

MUSIC WORK BOOKS

Our educational system has turned out such a profusion of work books for every subject, that most children have had quite enough of them by the time the school day is over. Filling in blanks or copying how to make a quarter note has so little to do with the wonderful experience of making a *sound* on the keyboard! To be sure, at some point in their musical education, the student should be exposed to writing notes, rests, treble and bass clef signs, and sharp and flat signs. However, I believe that children should be taught to make pleasing sounds on the keyboard before they are subjected to more written work.

A child who has expressed a desire for piano lessons can be quite dismayed to find that it involves yet another work book, where he employs a pencil and not his fingers on the keys. Occasionally a child will have a great desire for the written work. It has never happened to me, but certainly if a child had requested such a work book, I would have obtained it for him.

TEACHING THEORY

The written work associated with Music Theory can become extremely involved. During my many years of teaching piano, I met several high school students who had achieved the highest marks in the State Theory tests. Unfortunately, many of them could not *play* anything on the piano!

In general, I would recommend finding a teacher who concentrates on training the mind, eye, and fingers to produce sound from a piano, rather than a teacher who requires lots of written work. As students continue their piano studies, into college or conservatory, there is ample time to master the written work. Keyboard proficiency should come first. As noted before, theory is an integral part of well-taught scales, chords and technique.

NECESSITY FOR TEACHING TECHNIQUE

Far too many children are given a succession of little pieces, with no attention to the technical demands of more advanced piano material. They may become quite proficient at reading notes, and possibly counting the time correctly, but will be unable to perform a composition in the tempo intended. Lack of adequate technique stops a piano student from progressing.

Nothing can be accomplished on the keyboard without finger dexterity. A beginning student must be given keyboard exercises to train the individual use of each finger. As the student progresses, he should be taught triad chord positions — three notes struck at once with thumb, third and fifth fingers. Various positions of the three-tone chord will necessitate learning to use the second finger in the middle of a chord, as well.

As soon as possible, a student should be taught scales, in all octaves. The keyboard is five feet wide, and a pianist must be able to go from one end to the other with ease. Both the chromatic and whole-tone scales are the easiest to start with, and will give the young child a feeling of familiarity with the entire keyboard. More advanced students will learn arpeggios in various positions on the keyboard.

There are many excellent technique books available. For the younger student, it is desirable to see scales written in quarter notes. For the more advanced student, the Hanon technique books are the most satisfactory. Finger drills, trill drills, all the scales and arpeggios, plus complete cadences are printed in full. As the student develops into difficult piano literature, all scales should be taught and learned in thirds and sixths, as well as an octave apart, both hands together.

There is *no* substitute for adequate technique.

CHAPTER 16
PRACTICING

"Do I have to practice EVERY day?"

"I'll make it up on the weekend."

"If he plays that piece one more time I'll scream!"

"Does she HAVE to go over and over a measure?"

HOW LONG? HOW OFTEN?

Practicing must be done on a daily basis. Learning to play the piano does not lend itself to cramming a couple of days a week.

In the beginning, the very young student should practice 15 minutes a day. Hopefully, the parent will be an interested listener or companion. As the child learns more, he will resent any input from the parent. Gradually, a parent can shift to attentive listening two times a week. Eventually, the child will desire private practice, and will ask you to listen when he feels he has accomplished something worth hearing.

Depending on the child, the practice time should increase to 30 minutes daily quite soon, and then to one hour. Though one hour a day for an advanced student is not nearly enough, the daily hour is what most piano teachers must accept. Some students will want to do all their practicing at once. Others just can't accept that schedule at first, and break up the hour into segments.

Psychologists have noted that no one concentrates longer than 20 minutes at a time. An adult, or older student can blink his eyes or shift his body and continue his concentration another 20 minutes. The young student may need to get up, get a glass of water, or visit with you a moment before he can continue practicing.

The practice hour may be broken into several ideal segments. The first 20 minutes, perhaps before school, may be devoted to technique. The second 20 minutes, after school, may be on the study or sonata material. The last 20 minutes can be devoted to a solo and may be a break in between homework assignments for different school subjects.

There will be times when a student will really enjoy his practicing and extend the time much longer than the accustomed hour. If this happens, don't interrupt him. After a good hour of practicing, the student will discover how much better he can play when he is really warmed up.

THE PRACTICE SCHEDULE AND FAMILY COOPERATION

Both parent and student must adjust their time and priorities to allow for sufficient practice. If a compatible arrangement can be made in the home for the student to have a quiet, private practice session, there will be progress. This underlines the placement of the piano in the home, and the cooperative attitude of household members.

If the whole family is in an uproar with a certain practice plan, endeavor to find one that works with your family. Whatever plan you decide upon, make it possible for the student to adhere to it. Routine is the essence of good habits. The student can be brought to accept his practice sessions as easily as the time he goes to school.

Don't choose the time the child considers his most valuable. Usually this is directly after school, which may involve sports, plays, or clubs. Taking part in school activities is essential to the development of the individual. All children need a few minutes to 'run down' after school, and have a snack before piano practice begins.

Practicing can become an accepted and enjoyable part of a daily routine, with just a bit of help from the family. The courtesy of leaving the student alone, never calling out "you made a mistake!" and arranging family activities so the student knows that a definite time is his very own to use at the piano, are the ingredients of productive practicing. No one can practice if someone is constantly hovering over him, or people are dashing through the room.

In addition, courtesy and silence on the parent's part are very necessary. Parents, try to pretend you never heard a wrong note. Let the teacher correct it. Your relationship with your child will be far more pleasant if you do.

Don't make piano practice an either/or situation, or cause the child to miss a special event just to meet the schedule. Exceptions must be made from time to time to keep the child from hating piano, you, and the teacher. With a reasonable approach a child can lead a full school life, including social activities, as well as study, and still practice piano. Nothing will be gained, and perhaps a great deal will be lost, if a parent takes an inflexible stance on practice time.

Most teachers recognize that Sundays may present a home problem, and suggest that the student play through their full repertoire that day instead of playing or replaying only the lesson material.

MAKING PRACTICE TIME COUNT

A good teacher will show the student how to organize his lesson material for productive practicing. Practicing can be many things: boring, tiresome, exhilarating. But one thing it always is for any age— lonely. Learning to accept the time spent practicing the piano is a habit that evolves slowly over many years. Beginning students cannot practice as long as advanced students, who when studying difficult literature, can be delighted to put in two to four hours of intense concentration.

Playing straight through a piece is a fine beginning to a new composition. It gives an overview of the solo. Then the student should start learning the piece by musical divisions, such as a measure, a phrase, or a section. Learning two phrases a day of a piece will cover an enormous quantity of music, and the student can see and hear the accomplishment. Playing from beginning to end of a piece, day after day, with the same bad measures never improving, wastes time and is frustrating to the student.

Practice sessions should always accomplish something. At least one measure or phrase should be mastered daily so that the next day the student may add to that accomplishment. A teacher should show the student how to divide the lesson work into sections: e.g., technique—10 minutes; study piece—15 minutes; sonata—20 minutes; solo—15 minutes. These may be done one after the other or spread out over various times of the day. Certainly for a parent to force a child to sit at the piano for 60 minutes is totally non-productive.

If a clock or watch on the piano or in the room is going to reassure a student about his time commitment, by all means have it available. Our adult lives are controlled by the clock. Why shouldn't the piano student have the same courtesy of seeing how much or how little time he has practiced?

CHAPTER 17
LEARNING TO PERFORM

"Does he HAVE to play in a recital?"

"Will you excuse Scott just as soon as he has performed at the class? We have another engagement. "

"Mary Jane just can't attend the performance class, but she'll play in your recital, if she can make it. "

PERFORMANCE CLASSES

One recital a year is not enough training for the child to learn how to perform! A professional studio should provide monthly performance classes. These are training sessions for the young pianist. Usually they are held on a Saturday or Sunday afternoon in the studio. They should be for students only; no guests, no parents. If the teacher maintains a large studio, with a wide variety of age groups, there should be several programs scheduled according to age and proficiency.

Performance classes should be considered an extension of the private lesson. There is no other way to learn how to perform in public. Far too often because of intense stage fright and lack of practice, young performers will shamble onto a stage, play too hastily, forget to bow, and retreat off stage. It is so wrong for any teacher to put a child in such an embarrassing situation.

No qualified teacher would consider placing a child in a recital or public performance without some training in performance and stage deportment. One hour a month spent at a performance class will prepare your child to perform at a recital or other program. At such classes, a teacher will demonstrate how to approach the piano, arrange the bench, place the hands on the keyboard, locate the pedals, think a moment before playing, and how to take a proper bow and leave the stage.

A parent should recognize the importance of such monthly classes. They should never have a child rush in and inform the teacher he must play first so he can leave immediately to accommodate the family shopping plans. Attendance at a performance class for the entire time, is the only way a student may observe and learn from the other student's performances as well as his own.

There are innumerable benefits to having a child perform in front of his peers, and having this opportunity regularly on a monthly basis prepares the student for important recitals. All children know they will receive compliments (many times undeserved) from parents and grandparents. They also know that their peers are not so generous, and they will make a huge effort to play well at a class.

WHAT ARE THEY FOR?

A performance class is not a private lesson, nor is it a time when corrective or disparaging remarks are made by a teacher. Problems will be noted by the teacher, and discussed privately at the next lesson.

Students who are new to a studio should be invited to audit the first performance class. Perhaps they will need to attend more than one class before they feel confident enough to perform. I have never encountered a student who refused to participate after an opportunity to familiarize himself with a performance class procedure.

The first few performance classes will be very difficult for the student. He will be nervous, and probably will make several mistakes. He also will be learning how to control such situations, through additional practice and concentration. He will hear other students have difficulties, and this will encourage both him and the other students to try harder next time.

Unless you personally have performed in a program on a stage, you do not know how difficult it is! Remembering the proper way to enter a stage, perform intricate music with fingers and brain, try to make the music beautiful, take a bow, and leave the stage gracefully are skills that take practice. A teacher or studio that provides *only* one performance a year at a recital is not training your child to enjoy performing music. It is a cruel way to teach, and can result in a child refusing to continue his piano lessons.

MISTAKES ARE NOT FATAL

Every musician in the world, at some time, has heard one of the 'greats' get lost in a composition at a concert. Because they are professionals and have such awesome talents, they recover quickly and go on. The majority of the audience is unaware that anything was amiss. For the active pianists in the audience, they *know* what happened, but admire the smooth recovery and continuance.

Paderewski played wrong notes by the bucketful! Artur Rubenstein made errors many times in his performances, particularly in his younger years on stage. It never tarnished either pianist's reputation. They simply went on with great skill and panache.

As human beings, we make mistakes. With the less experienced performer, it will be more noticeable. However, it is not the mistake made in performance that is important. It is how the student handles the situation. The only way to learn how to get through such an experience is to have frequent performance opportunities.

RECITALS: ARE THEY NECESSARY?

Indeed they are! Recitals give both the student and teacher an opportunity to show what has been accomplished in a year of study. They are the "proof of the pudding" so to speak, that both student and teacher have achieved some goals.

The phrase "playing for one's own enjoyment" may sound good, but it isn't realistic. No one is going to enjoy playing badly whether alone or in front of an audience. One will never learn to play a composition well unless it is performed in front of someone else.

Recitals are wonderful experiences in more than just a musical sense. They help prepare the student to be an articulate and poised member of society. Recitals train him how to recover from a memory slip and proceed with dignity. They give the student the ability to share his talent with others who may not have musical skills, or who have not had the opportunity to study piano.

The well-prepared recital solo performance can be the highlight of the year, and perhaps a high point in your child's life. Preparation for this recital is greatly benefited by participation in monthly performance classes and performances at school or church.

THE PARENT'S CONTRIBUTION

A recital should be an *occasion*. The good piano teacher or studio will hold a recital in an adequate auditorium with a fine grand piano.

There should be printed programs. Non-performing students, who are new to the studio, or friends, may be asked to pass out programs at the door.

A teacher should expect the students to dress properly. Girls will look much better in a long skirt, even the younger girls. Considering the cost of clothing for growing children, I encouraged my girl students to buy a length of cotton print, sew up the sides, and gather the top. Worn with a plain blouse, it looks lovely on a stage. After the recital the skirt could be cut off and worn in the everyday wardrobe. Boys ideally will wear a suit or sport coat and slacks with shirt and tie. If this is a hardship on some families, a shirt and tie with long-sleeved pullover sweater can be an alternative. Short sleeve shirts should *never* be worn on a stage!

As a parent, help your child perform well by being a good audience. Charm bracelets, key rings and rustling programs can be very distracting. Very young brothers and sisters should be left at home. They are not able to stay quiet, and the young performer must be able to concentrate.

Some parents may want to add to the evening by assisting with refreshments. It is thoughtful and courteous of a teacher to introduce the graduating seniors from high school and mention their future plans. These are personal and optional additions to a recital.

ADDITIONAL PERFORMANCE OPPORTUNITIES

While the good piano teacher and studio *must* provide monthly performance classes, and a yearly recital, other performances should also be available for capable students. This will include State music contests, and high school music contests for pianists who are members of an orchestra or band with another instrument. There is always a division for the solo pianist, even though the high school contest emphasis is on ensemble performance.

A caring and inspired teacher will endeavor to find additional places for students to perform in his community. There are increasing numbers of residential homes for elderly people. Many of these facilities have a good grand piano, which *is a necessity* for performance. A child should *never* be scheduled to perform on a dreadful piano. The homes for senior citizens are an ideal place for a short program of five or six students. Many of these people cannot go to scheduled concerts where they live; either they lack transportation, or are too fragile to attend a function requiring a bus ride, and many steps. These audiences are very appreciative of both the music and the pleasure of seeing young people. Most communities have a woman's club that is receptive to scheduling an altruistic student program. Some church functions and services encourage the young, talented pianist to add to the beauty of the occasion by a solo performance.

For any student of piano, learning to share his abilities with others is not only part of character building, but a generous and happy activity. Not everyone has the talent or opportunity to learn to perform in public. The value of public performance is enormous. Playing piano in public is done *alone*. There is no partner, team, or committee to assist. This is a wonderful quality to add to your child's life; the ability to do something of value *all by himself*. The memory training, stage training and solo activity will help him be more successful in every aspect of his adult life.

CHAPTER 18
ENTERING COMPETITIONS

PROS AND CONS OF CONTESTS

Life is a contest. At some point in life, everyone must compete, whether it is for grades in school, piano contests, or a job. Learning how to compete, without letting it destroy you is a necessary lesson in life.

Contests are an important part of every piano student's instruction. They provide an incentive to a student to learn a solo thoroughly and perform well under stress. As traumatic as a contest can be, with the proper background, the child can benefit from being in a contest.

If a student is serious about piano study and intends to continue his study at university level, he must learn how to perform and compete in front of an audience. In order to be accepted as a piano student in any university or conservatory, he will be required to audition in front of members of the Piano Department. Even if the student has no intention of pursuing a musical career, either in college or after college, contest experiences can be of great value.

Rarely will a teacher enter *all* of his students in a contest. Some students are not proficient enough and some do not have the confidence to endure the stress. The advantage of participating in a contest is the opportunity for a student to see how well he can do under difficult circumstances. Also, he will receive a written critique by someone other than his teacher. Teachers and parents listen differently to a child than a stranger will listen. It can be helpful to student, teacher and parent to find out how the child sounds to someone else who is not involved with the child.

First and foremost for any contest is adequate preparation. A well-run studio will have provided the monthly performance classes, where the student can experience how well he plays under stressful conditions. There are many individuals who play beautifully when they are alone or at their lesson with only the teacher listening. An audience can make them so nervous that they are unable to do their best.

Just as there are those who thrive on the idea of competing, there are many young piano students who should *not* perform in contests. Those who are not competent enough to accept a critique, or those who are unable to conquer excessive nervousness, should not be forced into a contest. Both teacher and parent should listen to a pupil's preference. Do not force a child to compete if he is not ready. A contest should be a pleasant learning experience.

A parent must understand the pros and cons of contests, and decide, with the teacher's recommendation, if a contest is right for his child at that time. Perhaps at the early stages of piano study, he should not be entered, but as he progresses he may really want to enter. This must be a personal decision based on the child's ability and personality and the teacher's judgement.

TYPES OF CONTESTS

Many times the women's association supporting a symphony will sponsor a young artist contest. The prize for such a contest may include a performance with the symphony, as well as a monetary prize to be used for additional piano study. Musical organizations, both local and national, may sponsor a contest.

If the teacher is a member of the State Music Teachers Association, and any good teacher will be, he will be able to enter his students in the State Contest. This is the most common one open to students, although there are many other additional, local contests available in metropolitan areas.

Since state contests are the most common for a student to enter, knowledge of how they are held is important. At these contests, the student will play in a separate room with only the judge present. Neither the preliminary nor final contest judging is held before an audience. There will be a preliminary contest, followed by a final contest. The winners in the final contest usually are presented in a gala recital for an audience.

Students are divided into various age and difficulty levels. An appointed committee of the state organization will have prepared a list of appropriate solos for each grade category. A student may not compete in the same category more than one time. He must progress to the next age category to enter again. Usually there will be five or more selections in each category from which the teacher and student may choose a solo.

Obviously when students are playing different compositions within the same category, judging becomes a matter of personal opinion. The judge is not comparing how various students play the same piece, but different pieces. Every effort is made on the part of the teacher-judge to evaluate a performance as fairly as he can and write an encouraging evaluation.

ADVANCED CONTESTS

For the more gifted, and mature piano student, there are many opportunities to enter national contests. These are far more serious, as the result can be a scholarship to a conservatory, a substantial monetary prize for further study, or a contract to perform. The Leventritt, Van Cliburn, Tchaikovsky, and various contests held by music schools are just a few offered to the advanced pianist. These contests are judged by a panel of pianists and teachers, not just one judge. Usually there are definite compositions the pianist is required to perform and all contestants perform the same pieces. Most such contests demand the pianist play a variety of piano literature, ranging through Baroque, Classic, Romantic, Impressionistic and Contemporary. These competitions are for the pianist who is attempting to make his career as a performing artist.

WHO ARE THE JUDGES?

The judging of state contests is done by qualified members of the State Music Teachers Association. Each category will have its own judge. The teacher-judge will never judge his own students. A critique is written by the judge, and a numerical grade is given. The students with the highest grades will be allowed to compete in the final contest, which will be judged in the same manner. From these critiques and grades will be chosen the winners in each category.

Judges for state contests have attended training sessions where they are encouraged to phrase their opinions or corrections in terms that will not harm either the student or the teacher. All State Music Teacher Associations belong to the Music Teachers National Association which has helpful guidelines for state contests.

Most contests are not necessarily fair. A contest in a pure science like mathematics, where specific questions have exact answers, can be eminently fair. Contests in subjective subjects, whether music, poetry, art or literature, are judged on a wide and personal variety of criteria. Some judges will give their highest mark to the note-perfect performance. Other judges will be more influenced by the style in which a solo is performed. There will be some judges who consider the overall musicianship of the performances, even if it includes mistakes.

It is very difficult to be a judge. The student, teacher and parent may object strenuously to an opinion of a judge. However, when you enter a contest, you must be prepared to accept the judgement of another pianist. Judges are human beings and do make mistakes in evaluation, but certainly, they are doing their best.

LEARNING FROM CRITICISM

A student must be told repeatedly that a contest is an *experience* in learning. A teacher should stress the fact that failing to win high marks doesn't mean a student should abandon piano studies. Results of a contest are *one person's* opinion of how the student played a particular piece on a particular day. Most performers recognize they do not always play their best. Even the great artists are unhappy with some concerts, even though they have a wealth of experience playing for an audience.

All concerned need to remember that the judge is listening for a brief time to one solo. The teacher and parent may know what a triumph a performance has been for that child, but the judge hears the performance and considers it in relation to other contestants. If the child has been well prepared musically and mentally for a contest, another person's opinion may be put in perspective and be helpful. A child should never feel he has failed and that there will be another opportunity.

AN ALTERNATIVE TO CONTESTS

In many metropolitan areas, local piano teachers associations offer a performance opportunity to students of member teachers. These are excellent training sessions for students.

In Minneapolis, Minnesota where I taught piano for 21 years, a local organization, the Minneapolis Music Teachers Forum, presented bimonthly concerts during the school year. A teacher could present a limited number of students in each program. The chairman of that particular program would welcome the audience, explain how to approach the stage, arrange the bench, how to bow and leave the stage. The student was performing on a large grand piano on a stage. Usually one of the piano faculty from the University of Minnesota, or one of the many fine colleges in the Twin City area, would write an encouraging critique. It was an outstanding program, giving the student, parent and teacher an opportunity to experience a concert. After several performances at these Sunday concerts, a student gained enough confidence and experience to enter a contest.

Neither a teacher nor a parent should rush a child into public performance. But at some point, learning to share a talent with others is a necessity.

PART V: BEYOND THE BASICS

CHAPTER 19

THE LANGUAGE OF MUSIC

"I never could say that name . . . ha ha."

"Can he learn to play a Chopin Nectarine?"

"Why don't they just use plain English?"

A NOTE ON ORIGINS

The language of music must be considered a very important part of good piano instruction. Music, and the highly involved method of writing music on paper took several centuries to perfect. With its beginnings in Italy, musicians and copiers would use Latin as their language for words to church music, and for directions as to how it should be sung.

Through the centuries, before the printing press was invented and music could be reproduced rapidly, the main way that musical ideas were exchanged between different countries, was via the traveling troubadours. They shared what was popular in their various areas and added to their own knowledge by borrowing from the music of a new country.

It was only natural that Germans should add some of their words to the language of music, as the French added theirs. When music traveled across the Channel, English words appeared. Obviously a musician would need a working knowledge of several languages to comprehend the various titles and directions on copied or printed music. Since such ability is not common to the majority, a musical dictionary is a *must* for the piano student. Both words and correct pronunciations are essential to a well-trained musician.

LEARNING PROPER PRONUNCIATION

As well as having a large language of its own, music has been written by specific people who gave their compositions definite names. While the subject of correct pronunciation may seem trivial to some, the awful, often hilarious mispronunciations of composer's names or compositions are the fault of poor teachers who have neglected their obligation to teach correct pronunciation. An inexpensive music dictionary should be kept near the piano and a student should be encouraged to look up and find the meanings of words printed on music.

The most common words refer to tempo and style of compositions. Words such as *allegro, allegretto, andante, adagio,* and *presto* indicate the speed with which a piece is to be played. *Misterioso, tres leger, cantabile* and *rubato* refer to the style of a composition. Many compositions have titles that indicate the sort of solo it is, e.g., waltz, polonaise, minuet or march, or indicate a particular kind of piece, such as etude (study), nocturne (night music) or fantasy (a free form or semi-improvisational piece). These guidelines by the composer are of great value to the performer. The music dictionary takes the mystery out of these words and provides the student with the composer's concept of the music.

It is both respectful and knowledgeable to pronounce the title, composer and playing instructions correctly and should be a part of every lesson your child takes.

WHAT IS GREAT MUSIC?

In this book, you will read references to "great music" and "great composers." What does it mean?

I am going to reprint, by permission, excerpts from a fine editorial by Sydney J. Harris, about "Great Music." It may help to understand this marvelous field of piano music, and the lessons you and your child are about to undertake.

Artur Schnabel, the eminent concert pianist said: 'Great Music is music that is written better than it can be played.'

This is why popular songs, no matter how beguiling or lovely they might be, cannot be classified as 'great.' It is not a matter of snobbery, or tradition, or even craftsmanship in composing, but something far deeper that is difficult to put into words.

For an accomplished artist, it is easy to get out of a popular song everything the composer has put into it. But the most skilled musician in the world cannot exhaust the context of one of the late Beethoven piano sonatas, or a Mozart quartet.

No matter how 'faithfully' he plays it, there is always something beyond that eludes the definitive interpretation. Schnabel himself spent a professional lifetime trying to capture the essence of what Beethoven wrote. He came as close as anyone, but not to his satisfaction.

Moreover, each time the instrumentalist plays a piece of great music, he finds new meanings and nuances within, secrets that give themselves up only slowly and teasingly. However great his skill, he never succeeds in reproducing everything that was in the composer's intent. The 'ultimate performance' of a great composition is as out of reach as the ultimate production of 'Hamlet.'"

GREAT COMPOSERS AND PERFORMERS

Most people have never seen a picture of Bach when he was a young man. The common conception of the classical composers is that there were old men with beards. However Mozart, Mendelssohn, Liszt and Chopin were handsome young men when they were achieving fame.

Scholarly biographies of the older pianists are rarely read by students. Still young students and people interested in music appreciate finding out that the pianist composers were real, live people with personal problems and who experienced difficulties getting their careers started. The books available that illuminate us about the lives of these classic composers should be found and read.

We are fortunate that some of the contemporary "elder statesmen" of piano, such as Artur Rubenstein, Claudio Arrau and Vladimir Horowitz lived long enough to share their personalities with us. Harold C. Schonberg, music critic of the *New York Times* for many years, wrote a number of very entertaining books. His *The Great Pianists* should be read by every piano hopeful. *My Young Years* by Artur Rubenstein is a charming recital of a great pianist's life and career. Though not appealing to very young piano students, adult students will find them entertaining and informative.

Horowitz shared much of his life with the world public through television programs. He conducted himself on special programs with smiles and humor. Periodically, during television interviews, a reporter invariably asked him to play his difficult, bombastic arrangement of the "Stars and Stripes Forever." During World War II he made an altogether exciting and brilliant arrangement of that John Phillip Sousa march which he performed to enthusiastic audiences during those war years. Horowitz never lost his composure, but laughed, played a few bars and exclaimed, "It's too hard!" He endeared himself to the public by thus becoming a real, live virtuoso of the keyboard; one who could make mistakes and admit he was unable to remember it all.

A true musician will take delight in learning about the great composers of the past and present, and should make a career of reading books that illuminate the lives of these men. It is only hoped that more materials of this kind will become available to the younger pianists that will make those impressive names have a personality and inspire them to continue their studies.

CHAPTER 20
SOME FURTHER CONSIDERATIONS

"I had an uncle who could sit right down and play ANYTHING."

"Jane can play anything after hearing it once."

"Is improvising a lost art today?"

PLAYING FOR PLEASURE

Parents are providing piano lessons for their child because they want him to have the advantage of a musical education. They also want to hear music played in their homes. Many times a parent will have particular pieces he would love to have his child learn. These should be discussed with the teacher. If the child is advanced enough for a certain favorite piece, there is no reason why a teacher cannot assist the child to learn it.

A parent must recognize that practice on the assigned lesson must come first. If the child completes that work each day, there is no reason why additional music of his own choice cannot be enjoyed. A teacher has no right to dictate what a student plays in his free time.

The more music a student plays, the greater his chance to develop a facility in sight-reading, a taste for good music, and a desire to play more difficult pieces. As long as a student prepares his assigned lesson, he should be allowed to spend whatever additional time he wishes on whatever kind of music he wants. By widening his scope of music through more reading, the student will find that classical music can be quite fascinating and provide greater challenge than other kinds. Both parents and teachers should encourage a child to play additional music after their lesson material has been practiced.

This approach to piano lessons and practicing is much the same as that used by parents in the matter of books. If a parent keeps the home supplied with a large variety of library books and encourages the child to read, read, read, he will gradually develop a taste for well-written books. Not everything that is published is great literature, or even passable literature. Exposure to a wide selection develops the reading tastes and keeps a child reading.

So too with music. Playing quantities of music enhances the skill of the student, particularly sight-reading proficiency, and opens new areas of enjoyment. Keep several volumes like *Collections the Whole World Loves* on your piano. It can be of any variety you desire, but it is a good idea to stick with music that has been written expressly for piano. This will make piano lessons and the necessary practice less of a chore and more of a pleasurable musical experience.

PLAYING FOR PAY

Some students may want to continue the classical music route and possibly they will become professionals. Other students may want to spend more time with contemporary music, American jazz or country western. Fundamental training is necessary for skill in these avenues also, and many of the great popular musicians like Benny Goodman, Roger Williams and Peter Nero were initially trained in classical music.

As long as lesson material is practiced first, the child should be encouraged to read and play many types of piano music. Sight-reading, the ability to play through a solo, hymn or accompaniment that has not been practiced, can be a marketable skill. All instrumentalists require an accompanist to perform at their juries or solo performances. A competent sight-reader may place a notice on a bulletin board in the university music building or place his name on file with the music office. Many pianists have augmented their funds for college in this way.

SHOULD A STUDENT LISTEN TO RECORDS OR TAPES?

It is better not to listen to a tape or record of a composition prior to learning to play it. Trying to learn by imitation will result in copy work, not growth of musical knowledge.

I always encouraged my students to study a piece completely, a phrase at a time, to know the structure, style and concept of it, before ever listening to a recording of it. Taught properly thus, the student will listen with intelligent and critical ears. He may like some of the things an artist does, and he may dislike others.

Each of us is an individual. We must bring our own skills and talents to what we learn. If we simply attempt to imitate the thoughts of others, we obviously do not have sufficient thoughts of our own. Individual artists have their own style and concept of a particular composition, so that people can say with all honesty, "I like the way Ashkenazy plays this concerto better than I like the Byron Janis recording" or vice versa. There are definite differences in how music is performed and in individual reactions based on personal taste and knowledge.

HOW ABOUT IMPROVISING?

Many parents would love to have their children taught to improvise; that is, to be able to sit at the piano and tunefully doodle at the keyboard. Improvization is a skill and a gift that was extremely popular in the 18th and 19th centuries. Many of the great Baroque composers and performers improvised at the harpsichord to the delight of their patrons. Romantic pianists frequently included impromptu playing as part of their programs.

Today improvisation has almost totally disappeared from the concert stage. Victor Borge's very musical and clever spoofs at the keyboard are an example of excellent improvisation. In the past it was considered part of being a performing pianist to be able to improvise, although the skill has all but evaporated from the stage of serious performance.

Teachers of classical piano rarely incorporate this into their teaching since many cannot improvise themselves. The concept of improvisation can be explained and to some extent learned by a talented pupil. But on the whole, it isn't included in the lessons from classical teachers.

Certainly, improvisation is not for the very young student, and should not be an alternative to learning technique and written music. It is a refinement of an art, the rules of which must be studied first. Teachers who teach popular music teach the fundamentals of improvisation which require a thorough knowledge of key signatures, rhythmic patterns, chord structures, scale passages and special effects. There must be basic knowledge and fluency on the keyboard, plus a creative musical mind and a great deal of individual originality. Fine improvisation requires superb musicianship.

CHAPTER 21
SETTING REALISTIC GOALS

"Oh, I'll never teach!"

"He's more into composing than playing . . ."

"I want to be a concert pianist."

WHY IS HE TAKING PIANO LESSONS?

Most parents provide piano lessons for a child to enrich his life, develop what talent he has, and increase his knowledge in one of the great arts. If a child learns to play reasonably well and can participate in performance classes and a yearly recital, the parent will consider it has been a worthwhile investment. The majority of parents do not seriously believe their child will become a concert pianist.

There are the exceptional piano students who achieve great musicianship at an early age. Some of these *know* they want to study piano in college with the aim of performing and teaching on a university faculty. A student of such talent should be encouraged to perform a solo program at the end of junior high school and another when he graduates from senior high school.

Solo programs are large undertakings, but will give that talented pianist an opportunity to experience being the whole show. Programs of this nature require the cooperation of teacher and parent in the solo preparation, handling all the details involved in arranging for the auditorium, sending invitations, and having programs printed.

A student whose main aim in life is to be a concert pianist, should be reminded that there is very little room at the top. It is extremely difficult to become a well-known pianist and it requires not only superior ability, but many other factors. As with so many of the good things in life, extensive advanced training is expensive. There are hundreds of superb pianists in the U.S. today, few of whom will achieve fame. Of the fine pianists who place second, third or fourth in national and international contests, it can be hoped they will become the inspired artist-teachers at our universities and conservatories, performing a limited number of concerts each year.

The gifted pianist who insists he will never teach under any circumstances, places himself in an almost unemployable category. Our major symphony orchestras employ only *one* pianist. From a practical standpoint, all serious piano students must consider teaching as part of their lives. Since teaching at a conservatory or university requires at least a master's degree, his training and schooling must be planned accordingly.

ATTENDING A MUSIC CAMP

There are many excellent music camps throughout the U.S. that operate during the summer months. A few examples are Interlachan, Michigan; Marlboro, New Hampshire; and Aspen, Colorado. There are many more. The teaching staff of these summer camps are well known performing musicians and faculty members of conservatories and universities. The camps are very selective, expensive and demanding of the student. A student must be very good and very dedicated to benefit from such a high pressure situation.

Occasionally these experiences result in a scholarship to return the following summer or to attend a year at a conservatory. This is the rarity. The student will need the teacher's assistance in finding out the necessary information as to auditioning, in person or by tape, the cost, and the details of living quarters and expenses.

No teacher should encourage a mediocre student to attend a summer music camp. It requires great talent and the student must be mature and dedicated enough to gain from the experience. A good teacher will be honest with both student and parent as to a student's potential and whether it is worth the investment of both effort and money. *Very* rarely a young pianist might gain the ear to a well established pianist who *could* open doors for the young hopeful. This would be great good fortune.

The student and his parents must be realistic about hitching their wagon to the performing star. It is a rocky road. A more realistic goal for the fine piano student is to attempt to find employment on a university faculty or private music school, where he will teach and perform occasional concerts.

111

COMPOSITION AND ALTERNATIVE CAREERS

There are other careers open to the fine pianist and musician besides teaching. Some students may wish to pursue composition. Television and Hollywood need many of these talents. Every TV show has a music track that must be written or compiled by knowledgeable musicians. Radio stations need program directors who select compositions and programs to be broadcast. Music therapy has become a university subject and is used to treat mentally disturbed patients and autistic children.

We live in a world that devours talent and entertainment on a grand scale. Our civilization wants to be amused and entertained, and that requires music. Some serious piano students may eventually find a place the world of popular music. Certainly our popular musicians out-earn many of the classical soloists.

The percentage of students who will make it to the concert stage, whatever medium of music they choose, is very small. It is unrealistic to study piano with only a concert career in mind. Just as there is only one Mozart and one Horowitz, few can expect to reach a position equal to theirs. Most of the famous classical performers have rocketed to fame by age 16; most popular performers are established by the time they reach their 20's.

Parents and teachers must encourage and support the dreams of the young musician, but not raise false hopes. The spotlight focuses on such a very few.

CONCLUSION

Giving your child the privilege of piano lessons is a gift that will be appreciated by him all his life. Besides allowing him the joy of learning and playing beautiful music, you will have exposed him to many disciplines valuable to his overall development. Playing the piano well is a fascinating and rewarding experience. Your efforts as a parent to provide the best teacher you can find, the best instrument you can afford, and all the encouragement possible, will provide him with a lifetime companion. Music is the greatest of the arts, and the piano is the most sublime instrument created by man.

ABOUT THE AUTHOR

Mary Teel Johnson grew up in the State of Washington, attending Washington State University, where she completed degrees in Music Education and Piano Performance. Advanced study was done with Silvio Risegari and Paul Pierre McNeely, of Seattle, Washington, and Marcia Emerson Weiser of Minneapolis, Minnesota. Master's work was done with Madame Rosina Lhevinne of Juilliard, at the Los Angeles Conservatory, Los Angeles, California.

She has taught 45 years as a private piano teacher, primarily teaching teenage students. She has been a member of the Washington State Music Teachers Association, the California Music Teachers Association, the Minnesota Music Teachers Association, and the Music Teachers National Association.

While living in Minneapolis, Minnesota, she was a performing artist member of The Thursday Musical, and the Schubert Club. Mary Teel Johnson is a life member of Mu Phi Epsilon music fraternity and Phi Kappa Phi scholastic honorary. At present, she is retired and living with her husband in Monterey, California.